US Citizenship Test Study Guide 2024

Master the Naturalization Exam with A Complete Study Guide for the USCIS Civics Test with Over 100 Practice Questions and Answers

By

Dustin Parkin

TABLE OF CONTENT

INTRODUCTION

The United States Citizenship Test, often known as the USCSI (U.S. Citizenship and Immigration Services) test, is an essential component of the naturalization process for those seeking U.S. citizenship. The purpose of the exam is to evaluate an applicant's knowledge of American history, culture and government, to ensure that they have a fundamental grasp of the country they wish to join.

The US Citizenship Test comprises multiple-choice questions regarding American history, government, and culture. Exam themes include the principles and ideals of American democracy, the organization of the U.S. government, the history of the country, and significant historical personalities and events. Questions are chosen from a pool of one hundred questions and are meant to assess a person's knowledge on a range of difficulty levels.

The exam is normally offered in English, although persons with poor English proficiency may get accommodations, such as the employment of a translator or the provision of the test in other languages. To pass the US Citizenship Test, candidates must properly answer at least six of ten questions.

In addition to completing the US Citizenship Test, persons must fulfill additional eligibility requirements for naturalization, including a specified duration of continuous residency in the

United States, high moral character, and the ability to speak, read, and write basic English.

The US Citizenship Test is an essential instrument for ensuring that those who become U.S. citizens have a fundamental knowledge of the country's ideals and principles. It is meant to examine a candidate's knowledge of American history, government, and culture, as well as their comprehension of the principles and ideals that distinguish the United States.

The examination questions span a broad variety of topics and are meant to be both exhaustive and difficult. Individuals may be questioned about the branches of the

United States government, the Bill of Rights, and significant historical persons and events, among other topics. In addition, they may be asked about the rights and obligations of U.S. citizens, such as the right to vote, the right to free expression, and the duty to serve on a jury if summoned.

The US Citizenship Test is an integral part of the naturalization procedure and is designed to guarantee that persons who become U.S. citizens have a fundamental grasp of the country and its values and ideals. Individuals have the chance to display their patriotism and understanding of American history, government, and culture.

In conclusion, the US Citizenship Test is a crucial component of the naturalization procedure for those seeking U.S. citizenship. It is meant to evaluate an applicant's knowledge of American history, government, and culture and to ensure that they have a fundamental understanding of the country they wish to join. Individuals can demonstrate their loyalty to the United States and their understanding of its history, government, and culture by passing the exam.

CHAPTER 1: CITIZENSHIP AND NATURALIZATION EXAMINATION

The U.S. has a long tradition of embracing immigrants from throughout the globe. The United States honors the contributions of immigrants, who continue to enhance the country and uphold its heritage as a place of liberty and opportunity. USCIS is proud of its role in preserving America's legacy as a nation of immigrants and will deliver immigration and naturalization benefits with honesty.

Citizenship in the United States is a unique link that binds individuals around civic values and confidence in the rights and liberties provided by the U.S. Constitution. The promise of citizenship is based on the fundamental belief that all people are created equal and acts as a uniting identity to ensure that people of all backgrounds, whether native-born or foreign-born, have an equal interest in the future of the United States.

1.1 Becoming A U.S. Citizen

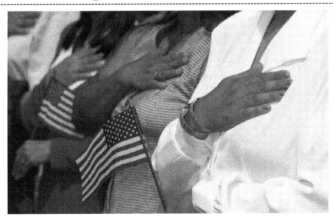

Obtaining U.S. citizenship requires multiple procedures, including completing specific qualifying conditions, filing an application, undergoing an interview, and clearing an examination.

A person must first possess a green card for at least 5 years or 3 years if they are married to a U.S. citizen. In addition, they must be at least 18 years old, capable of reading, writing, and speaking English and have a fundamental knowledge of American history and government. In addition, they must be of excellent moral character and have continually lived in the United States for a period of time.

Once eligibility has been determined, the applicant must complete and submit Form N-400, together with supporting paperwork and applicable costs. The application asks, among other things, about the applicant's personal history, immigration status, and criminal record.

Upon application submission, an interview with a USCIS official will be scheduled. The officer will study the applicant's application and ask important questions about their background and immigration history during the interview.

After the interview, the candidate must pass a citizenship exam consisting of questions regarding U.S. history, government, and English skills. The purpose of the exam is to ensure that the candidate has a fundamental grasp of the United States and is able to act as a citizen.

The individual will be scheduled for a ceremony when they will swear an oath of loyalty to the United States and obtain their Certificate of Naturalization, formally awarding them U.S. citizenship, assuming they pass the examination.

1.2 USCIS Authority to Naturalize

It is well-established that Congress has the unique constitutional ability to set a consistent system of naturalization and to pass legislation that confers citizenship to individuals. Prior to 1991, naturalization in the United States was a judicial activity carried out by several courts specified by acts established by Congress according to its constitutional authority to establish a standard rule of naturalization.

Congress handed naturalization jurisdiction to the Attorney General on October 1, 1991. USCIS is allowed to carry out all actions required to effectuate the Secretary's authority. In some instances, a naturalization applicant may choose between having the Oath of Allegiance given by USCIS or a court with authority. Courts that qualify may elect to have the sole power to administer the Oath of Allegiance.

1.3 Naturalization Examination

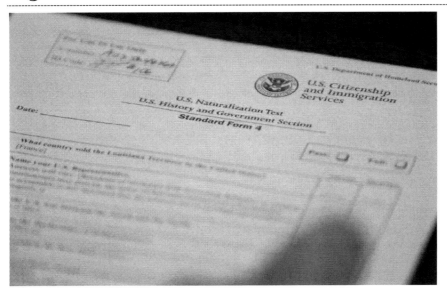

Purpose

The naturalization examination, often known as the citizenship test, is designed to evaluate an applicant's knowledge of the U.S. government, history, and the English language, as well as their devotion to the ideals and principles of the United States.

Applicants for naturalization must pass the citizenship exam, which consists of 2 parts: a civics examination and an English language test. The civics exam evaluates the applicant's understanding of American history and governance, including the Bill of Rights, the Constitution, and the branches of government. This test evaluates the applicant's abilities to write, read, and speak English.

The purpose of the naturalization examination is to guarantee that persons who become U.S. citizens have a fundamental grasp of the U.S. government and history, as well as strong English communication skills. This is necessary to fully participate in American culture and to use the rights and advantages of U.S. citizenship.

The naturalization examination also involves an interview with a U.S. Citizenship and Immigration Services (USCIS) officer, who will evaluate the applicant's application and ask questions about their immigration history, background, and other pertinent information.

Overall, the objective of the naturalization exam is to guarantee that persons who become U.S. citizens are well-informed, devoted members of American society who can actively engage in the country's civic life and contribute to the country's democracy.

Background

In the United States, the naturalization examination, often termed the citizenship test, has a lengthy history. As part of a larger attempt to restrict and manage immigration to the United States, the first citizenship exam was administered in 1906.

At the time, the citizenship test consisted of only a handful of questions regarding U.S. history and government. In order to guarantee that those who become U.S. citizens have a fundamental grasp of the country's history, governance, and ideals, the exam has been broadened and altered throughout time to reflect changes in American culture.

In 1952, Congress approved the Immigration and Nationality Act, which established the present naturalization procedure and made the citizenship exam mandatory for all U.S. citizenship applicants. In 2006, the test was redesigned with a new emphasis on civic awareness and the significance of English language skills.

Background Investigation

US Citizenship and Immigration Services (USCIS) performs a background check on all applicants for U.S. citizenship as part of the naturalization process. The goal of the inquiry is to discover if the applicant fits the eligibility conditions for naturalization and to analyze their appropriateness for U.S. citizenship.

Typically, the background check involves a study of the applicant's immigration status and criminal record, as well as their personal history and character. USCIS may also conduct interviews with the candidate, the applicant's family members, and other persons who can offer background information.

Here are some of the most important processes involved in doing a background investigation:

Biometric collection: As part of the naturalization process, USCIS obtains the applicant's fingerprints and other biometric data, such as pictures, which are used to perform a background check with the FBI and the Department of Homeland Security, among others. Biometrics are used to confirm the applicant's identity and examine any criminal or immigration record that may be related to that identity.

Criminal history check: USCIS investigates the applicant's criminal background in the United States and other countries where they have resided. This involves checking for criminal records in state, federal, and local law enforcement databases, as well as international databases via international cooperation agreements. USCIS may also investigate police reports, court records, and other pertinent documents to determine if the applicant's criminal background disqualifies them for citizenship.

Immigration history check: USCIS examines the applicant's immigration history, which includes lawful entrance to the United States, compliance with immigration rules, and any prior immigration offenses. To verify the applicant's immigration history, USCIS may check the applicant's prior visa applications, I-94 Departure/Arrival Records, and other immigration-related documentation.

Personal interview: The applicant may be interviewed by USCIS to explain their background, immigration history, and other pertinent information. The interview is a chance for USCIS to inquire about the applicant's background and check the information supplied on the application. USCIS may also conduct interviews with the applicant's relatives, employers, and other persons who can give more information about the application.

Security checks: USCIS performs a number of security investigations on the applicant, including inspections of terrorist watchlists, criminal database records, and other government records. USCIS may also utilize advanced screening technologies, such as face recognition and biometric matching, to authenticate the applicant's identification and identify potential security concerns.

The purpose of the background investigation is to guarantee that persons who become U.S. citizens are qualified for naturalization and that they do not constitute a threat to public safety or national security. It may take some months to complete, but it is a crucial stage in the naturalization procedure.

1.4 Naturalization Interview

The Naturalization Interview is a crucial stage in attaining United States citizenship via the USCIS Naturalization Test. The goal of the interview is for the USCIS official to assess your application and certify that you fulfill all naturalization eligibility conditions. During the interview, you will be questioned about your personal history, your background, and English language and American government and history expertise.

Here is what you may expect during the interview for naturalization:

Review of your application: The USCIS officer will evaluate your N-400 application and any related supporting materials.

They will request that you verify the application information and supply any extra information they may want.

English proficiency test: You will be needed to show your ability to write, read, and speak basic English during the interview. The USCIS officer will tell you to read an English sentence and write an English sentence.

Civics test: The USCIS officer will ask you 10 of the 100 questions you prepared for in the Civics examination. You must answer at least 6 of the 10 questions correctly.

Background questions: The USCIS officer will inquire about your family, job, and travel history, among other topics. They may also inquire about your community ties and adherence to the ideas of the United States Constitution.

Oath of Allegiance: If you successfully complete the Naturalization Interview, the USCIS official will deliver the Pledge of Allegiance. This is the final stage in the naturalization process; once you have taken the oath, you will become a U.S. citizen.

Tips

Here are some pointers on how to prepare for and what to anticipate during the naturalization interview.

Examine the English language, U.S. government, and American history: Ensure that you have a solid grasp of the English language, as well as the concepts and structure of the United States government and its history. You can utilize the study materials and resources provided by USCIS to prepare.

Collect supporting documentation: Bring any supporting documentation that you provided with your N-400 application in its original form. This may include a legitimate photo ID issued by the government, your marriage certificate, or your tax returns.

Dress accordingly: Dress modestly and nicely for the interview. Avoid wearing apparel with distracting, political, or religious logos or slogans.

Arrive promptly: Arrive at the USCIS office at least thirty minutes before your planned interview time. This will provide you with sufficient time to park and clear security.

Be prepared for queries about your background: You may be questioned about your personal background, including family, job, and travel details. Be prepared to respond to questions on your commitment to the values of the U.S. Constitution and your links to your community.

Focus on the inquiries: During the interview, pay close attention to the USCIS officer's inquiries and provide genuine, competent responses. Clear your speech and utilize good English.

Be Respectful: Regard the USCIS officer with courtesy and respect. The officer should be addressed as "ma'am" or "sir". Avoid interrupting the officer or speaking aggressively or loudly.

Speak clearly: When answering questions, speak clearly and use proper English. Make eye contact with the USCIS officer and show that you are focused and attentive.

Be honest: Answer the USCIS officer's questions truthfully and to the best of your ability. Do not try to hide or conceal information. If you are unsure of an answer, simply say so and provide the best answer that you can.

Show your knowledge: Demonstrate your knowledge of the English language, U.S. government and history, and your commitment to the principles of the U.S. Constitution. Be prepared to answer questions about your personal history, including information about your family, employment, and travel.

Be confident: Be confident and positive in your responses. Show that you are excited about becoming a U.S. citizen and that you are prepared to take the Oath of Allegiance.

Stay Calm: The Naturalization Interview might be nerve-racking, but you should remain composed and focused. Keep in mind that the USCIS officer is there to assist you and assess your application.

Be Patient: completing the Naturalization Interview process might take many months. Be patient and maintain communication with the USCIS office to verify that your application is being accurately handled.

By adhering to these guidelines, you may guarantee that your Naturalization Interview goes as planned and that you are well-prepared to become a citizen of the United States.

1.5 Results of the Naturalization Examination

The United States Citizenship and Immigration Services (USCIS) will decide the applicant's eligibility for U.S. citizenship following the naturalization exam. The USCIS will mail a notification of its decision to the applicant. Here is a more thorough description of what occurs following the results of the naturalization exam:

The candidate will get an invitation to a ceremony when they take the Oath of Allegiance and become a U.S. citizen if they pass the naturalization examination. The invitation will mention the ceremony's date, time, and venue. The ceremony is normally held between 45 and 180 days after the candidate takes the naturalization exam. It is a ceremonial occasion in which the applicant pledges loyalty to the United States and the Constitution.

In rare instances, the USCIS may require more processing before rendering a determination on a naturalization application. This may happen if the applicant's history or identity cannot be verified. In such circumstances, USCIS may seek further information or paperwork from the applicant in order to resolve any difficulties.

If the USCIS concludes that the applicant is not qualified for U.S. citizenship, they will write a rejection letter outlining the grounds for the decision. The applicant can demand a hearing with an immigration officer to evaluate the decision or file an appeal through the federal court system. The refusal letter will detail the exact grounds for the decision, such as a criminal background or failing to satisfy the naturalization residence criteria.

If the candidate fails the citizenship exam, USCIS will notify them of their re-examination date. Typically, the re-examination will be scheduled 60 to 90 days after the original test. To boost their chances of passing the examination, the candidate will need to prepare for the test once more.

If the applicant has an immediate need for U.S. citizenship, the USCIS may conduct an accelerated oath ceremony in certain instances. Military deployments and medical emergencies are examples of urgent demands. If the applicant has a strong basis for requesting an accelerated oath ceremony, they may contact

USCIS and request one. The USCIS will analyze the request and decide if the expedited ceremony may be granted.

In conclusion, the procedure after the naturalization test might differ based on the circumstances of the applicant. The candidate will attend a special ceremony to take the Oath of Allegiance and become a U.S. citizen if they pass the examination. If extra processing or paperwork is required, the USCIS will contact the applicant to seek additional information. The candidate may reschedule the exam to take it again if they do not pass. The applicant has the option of requesting a hearing or appealing the judgment if the application is refused. In rare instances, candidates with urgent requirements may be eligible for an accelerated oath ceremony.

1.6 Motion to Reopen

A Motion to Reopen is a request to the USCIS to reopen a decision on an immigration application or petition. This motion is typically filed when new evidence or circumstances arise that were not available at the time of the original decision. In the context of the US citizenship test, a Motion to Reopen may be filed if the applicant's naturalization application was denied due to a failure to pass the examination.

1.7 USCIS Hearing

Hearing Request

A candidate or his/her designated agent may seek a USCIS hearing prior to an official over the refusal of an application for citizenship. The applicant or authorized agent must submit the request to USCIS within 30 days of receiving the refusal notification.

Review of Promptly Filed Request for Hearing

1. Scheduled Hearing within 180 Days

USCIS schedules a hearing between 180 days of receiving a timely request for a hearing. The hearing must be held by a different officer from the one who administered the first examination or who declined the application. The officer handling the hearing must be of an equivalent or higher grade than the officer administering the examination.

2. Review of Application

An officer may perform a de novo assessment of the applicant's naturalization application or a less formal review process based on the following criteria:

- The difficulty of the problems to be examined or resolved; and

- The necessity of completing additional naturalization-required tests.

A de novo review indicates that the officer conducts a fresh and comprehensive evaluation of the naturalization application.

An officer handling the hearing has the discretion and power to:

- Review all parts of the naturalization application and reexamine the applicant;

- Review any records, files, or reports prepared as part of the examination.

- Receive fresh evidence and testimony pertinent to the individual's eligibility; and

- Affirm the prior officer's refusal in whole or in part, or re-determine the decision.

The officer presiding over the hearing:

- Validates the facts in the rejection and upholds the original judgment to refuse;

- Reconsiders the previous decision but rejects the application based on newly found reasons of ineligibility; or

- Reconsiders the initial decision, reverses the previous denial, and grants the application for citizenship.

3. Testing of English and Civics at Hearing

In naturalization hearings involving applications refused for not meeting the educational criteria (Civics and English), officers must retake any section of the Civics or English exams that the applicant failed before. At the hearing, officers offer just one chance to clear the failed portion of the examinations.

CHAPTER 2: TEST FORMAT

The US Citizenship Test is a component of the naturalization procedure for those seeking U.S. citizenship. The test evaluates the applicant's English proficiency and knowledge of the American government, history, and civics. The format of the exam is as follows:

1. **English Test:** The candidate must demonstrate proficiency in reading, writing, and speaking English. They will be required to read and write a single sentence in English.

2. **Civics Test:** The Civics Exam consists of ten questions chosen from a pool of one hundred. The questions will include themes such as the fundamentals of the Constitution, American democracy, the Bill of Rights, and the roles of the government's branches. During the examination, the candidate must properly answer at least six of ten questions.

A USCIS official administers the US Citizenship Test. The test is administered orally and is administered in English. Complete the examination in around 10 to 20 minutes.

Notably, USCIS may make exceptions for candidates who cannot take the test owing to a developmental or physical impairment or medical condition. In addition, USCIS may administer the exam in a language other than English if the candidate cannot comprehend or communicate in English.

Applicants are recommended to review the official USCIS study guides and the possible 100 questions on the Civics Test in order to prepare for the exam.

A candidate has two chances to clear the English and civics examinations: the first test and the re-examination interview. After two attempts, USCIS refuses the naturalization application if the candidate fails to pass any element of the examinations. In circumstances when an applicant asks for a USCIS hearing over a rejection, officials are required to administer any failed exams.

Failure to present at the re-examination for testing or to take the examinations at an examination or hearing, unless excused by USCIS, qualifies as a failed attempt to pass the test.

2.1 English Test

A candidate for naturalization must merely demonstrate the ability to write, read, speak, and comprehend language in common usage. Ordinary use denotes intelligible and relevant communication using simple grammar and vocabulary, which may have glaring faults in pronouncing, building, spelling, and comprehending particular phrases, words, and sentences.

A candidate may request that phrases be rephrased or repeated and may make certain mistakes in spelling, pronunciation, and grammar and yet fulfill the naturalization criterion for English. The officer should repeat and restate inquiries until he or she determines that the applicant either completely comprehends the question or cannot understand English.

Speaking Test

An officer evaluates a candidate's capability to communicate and understand English depending on the candidate's ability to reply to questions often posed during the naturalization examination. The officer's inquiries pertain to eligibility and include inquiries from the application for naturalization. During the naturalization examination, the officer must rephrase and repeat questions until he or she is convinced that the candidate neither comprehends the inquiries or does not comprehend English.

The applicant must be able to speak in English regarding his or her application and suitability for naturalization if he or she does not qualify for an exemption from the English requirement. A candidate is not required to comprehend every word and sentence on the application.

Passing the Speaking Test

If the applicant understands and replies meaningfully to questions regarding his or her eligibility for citizenship, then he or she has proven acceptable English proficiency.

Failing the Speaking Test

A candidate fails the speaking exam if he or she does not comprehend enough English to be brought under oath or to respond to the eligibility queries on the application for citizenship. The officer must continue to administer the other sections of the naturalization exam, including the writing, reading, and civics sections.

An official cannot propose or accept the withdrawal of an application from a non-English-speaking applicant unless the applicant is accompanied by an interpreter who can explain the ramifications of withdrawing the application.

Reading Test

To demonstrate appropriate reading proficiency in English, candidates must read one out of 3 sentences. The officer administers the reading exam utilizing reading test forms. After the applicant properly reads one of the 3 phrases, the officer terminates the reading exam.

Passing the Reading Test

A candidate passes the reading exam if he or she reads 1 of the 3 sentences without long pauses in such a way that the content of the sentence is conveyed and the officer understands the text. In general, the candidate must read all words of content but may skip smaller phrases or make intonation or pronunciation faults that do not compromise the meaning.

Failing the Reading Test

A candidate fails the reading exam if he or she cannot read at least 1 of the 3 sentences correctly. A candidate fails to correctly read a phrase if he or she:

- Pauses for lengthy periods of time throughout the reading; or

- Excludes a content word or replaces another term for a content word;

- Uses incorrect pronunciation or intonation to the degree that the applicant cannot express the intended meaning of the statement and the officer cannot comprehend the sentence.

Writing Test

To adequately show the capacity to write in English, the candidate must compose one of three phrases in a way that the officer can comprehend. The officer dictates the phrase using standardized writing exam forms to the applicant. A candidate may not shorten any of the terms. The officer terminates the writing exam whenever the applicant has written 1 of the 3 sentences in a way that the officer can comprehend.

A candidate does not fail the writing exam because of mistakes in capitalization, spelling, or punctuation unless the flaws interfere with the sense of the statement and the officer cannot comprehend it.

Passing the Writing Test

The candidate qualifies for the writing exam if he or she can express to the officer the meaning of 1 of the 3 phrases. The applicant's sample of writing may include the following:

- A few spelling, grammatical, or capitalization problems;

- Excluded small words that do not significantly alter the content; or

- Numbers are written with or without digits.

Failing the Writing Test

A candidate fails the writing exam if his or her mistakes are so severe that the meaning of the sentence cannot be conveyed, and the officer cannot comprehend the sentence.

A candidate fails the writing examination if he or she writes any of the following:

- Different phrases or words;

- An abbreviation for a given word;

- Nothing or 1 or 2 isolated words; or

- An incomprehensible statement.

2.2 Civics Test

Typically, the US Citizenship Civics Test consists of only 10 questions picked at random from a pool of 100 questions. Providing a 2000-word response is neither practicable nor required. Here is a quick summary of the test's components:

- A foundational understanding of the United States government and its checks and balances system.

- Knowledge of the rights and duties of citizenship, especially the freedoms of religion, expression, and the press.

- Understanding of the US political structure, including the functions of the president, legislature, and judiciary.

- Awareness of American public holidays and symbols such as the national song and the flag.

- Knowledge of the important events in US history, such as the Civil War and the American Revolution.

- Understanding of the United States geography, including its territories, states, and capitals.

- Knowledge of significant historical documents, such as the Declaration of Independence and the Constitution.

- Understanding of the significance of civic involvement and voting in a democratic country.

- Understanding of the naturalization procedure and prerequisites for gaining US citizenship.

- Awareness of the obligations of US residents, such as jury duty, tax payment, and registration for the draft.

It is vital to note that the exam questions are meant to evaluate the applicant's English comprehension and communication skills, as well as their understanding of American history and government. The examination is intended to be difficult but achievable, and candidates are urged to prepare and study in advance.

2.3 Failure to Meet The Civics Or English Requirements

If a candidate fails any component of the civics test, the English test, or all tests during the original naturalization examination,

USCIS reschedules the candidate to take a second examination between 60 and 90 days following the initial examination.

In instances when the candidate presents for a reexamination, the reexamining supervisor must not give the identical civics or English test forms as during the first exam. Officers are only required to retest applicants in areas where they previously failed. For instance, if the candidate cleared the English reading, speaking, and civics aspects of the original examination but failed the writing component, the officer must administer only the English writing portion at the re-examination.

If an applicant fails any section of the naturalization exam a second time, the examiner must decline the application based on the applicant's failure to complete the naturalization education requirements. In the refusal notice, the officer must also address any additional areas of ineligibility. The applicant fails to fulfill the educational criteria if he or she refuses to be tested, refuses to reply to particular questions on the writing, reading, or civics exam, or is unable to respond to qualifying questions since he or she did not comprehend the questions as stated or rephrased. The officer should consider a candidate's unwillingness to be tested or to answer test questions as a test failure.

2.4 Documenting Test Results

All officers giving the English and civics examinations must record the test results in the applicant's A-file. Officers are obligated to complete and give each applicant the findings of the naturalization testing and examination at the conclusion of the examination unless the officer provides the applicant with a rejection notice at that time. The outcomes of the examination comprise the outcomes of the civics and English examinations.

CHAPTER 3: 100 USCSI Q&A EXPLANATION

The one hundred questions and answers on civics (government and history) of the citizenship exam are provided here. The civics examination is an oral examination, and the USCIS officer would ask the candidate up to ten of the one hundred questions. To clear the civics component of the citizenship exam, a candidate must properly answer six of ten questions. Due to elections or appointments, certain naturalization exam answers may change. As you prepare for the exam, ensure that you are familiar with the most recent responses to these questions.

Here are the 100 USCSI Q&A with explanations:

3.1 American Government

A: Principles of American Democracy

Question 1: What is the role of the Constitution?

Explanation: This inquiry pertains to the purpose and function of the Constitution of the United States of America, the supreme law of the nation.

The Constitution describes the organization and functions of the federal government, as well as the rights and protections granted to citizens and noncitizens. It describes the powers and responsibilities of the three branches of government (executive, legislative, and judiciary) and establishes their distinct roles.

The Constitution also outlines the mechanism for modifying the constitution, ensuring that it may adapt to the changing demands of the nation and its population throughout time.

The Constitution serves as the basis for the system of governance in the United States and is a cornerstone of democratic ideas and values. As such, it is an essential component of the US citizenship exam, as it ensures that new citizens have a fundamental grasp of the country's laws, governance, and history.

Question 2: What is meant by the term "amendment"?

Explanation: A constitutional or legislative amendment is a change or addition to the original document. In the context of the U.S. Constitution, an amendment is a formal change to the original text that must be ratified by a specific number of states prior to becoming part of the Constitution. There are 27 amendments to the U.S. Constitution, which serve to extend and protect the rights of the American people and clarify different areas of government administration.

Question 3: Self-government is mentioned in the first 3 words of the Constitution. What do these terms mean?

Explanation: "We the People" are the opening three words of the Constitution of the United States of America. These phrases reflect the essential concept of self-government, which is the

basis of the democratic system in the United States. The phrase "We the People" symbolizes that the ultimate authority of government in the United States is with the people and that the Constitution was created to serve the people and defend their rights and liberties.

The concept of self-governance is a crucial part of the US citizenship exam, as it serves to ensure that new citizens comprehend the concepts and ideals upon which the country was formed, as well as the role they play in sustaining and protecting its democratic system of government. Understanding the importance of "We the People" is vital for comprehending the Constitution's purpose and operation and for engaging in American democracy as educated and involved citizens.

Question 4: How do you describe the supreme law in the land?

Explanation: The question refers to the highest court in the United States of America. The answer is the Constitution of the United States of America, which acts as the ultimate law and defines the structure of the federal government as well as the rights and protections of citizens and noncitizens.

Question 5: What do we name the first 10 Constitutional amendments?

Explanation: The first 10 amendments of the United States Constitution are referred to together as the "Bill of Rights."

These amendments were introduced to the Constitution in 1791 to preserve individual rights, especially freedom of religion, the press, speech, and the right to keep and bear weapons, among others. The Bill of Rights continues to be a pillar of American democracy and is regarded as one of the most significant texts in American history.

Question 6: How many amendments are there to the Constitution?

Explanation: The United States Constitution contains 27 amendments in all. The first 10 (known as the "Bill of Rights") amendments were added in 1791, while the most recent, the 27th Amendment, was added in 1992. The amendments extend and safeguard the rights of American individuals, clarify different facets of the government's operation, and form the basis for a truly functioning democracy.

Question 7: What is one liberty or right guaranteed by the First Amendment?

Explanation: Freedom of speech is one of the rights or liberties granted by the 1st Amendment of the United States Constitution. This implies that American individuals are free to share their beliefs and ideas without fear of reprisal or censorship from the government. Freedom of expression is widely regarded as one of the most essential rights guaranteed by the Constitution and a pillar of American democracy. In addition to protecting free speech, the 1st Amendment also protects freedom of the press, freedom of religion, and the right to assemble peacefully.

Question 8: What was the purpose of the Declaration of Independence?

Explanation: The Independence Declaration was a declaration adopted on July 4, 1776, by the Continental Congress during the American Revolution. It proclaimed the independence of the thirteen American colonies from British control and affirmed their right to establish a new nation. Thomas Jefferson wrote the Declaration, which was motivated by Enlightenment concepts of personal rights and government authority. The letter served as a formal declaration of the colonies' complaints against the British Crown and aided in galvanizing support for the revolutionary cause. The Declaration of Independence is widely considered a cornerstone of American democracy and remains an essential emblem of American independence.

Question 9: What is the United States' economic system?

Explanation: The United States' economic system is a capitalist mixed economy. This indicates that it is a market economy in which services and goods are created and traded in accordance with the rules of supply and demand. However, it also involves government engagement and regulation in key sectors, such as education and health care. High levels of private enterprise, low rates of government control and ownership and a strong heritage of entrepreneurship and innovation characterize the U.S. economy. Despite experiencing phases of expansion and contraction, the U.S. economy remains one of the biggest and most dynamic in the world.

Question 10: What is religious freedom?

Explanation: Religion is a basic freedom guaranteed by the 1st Amendment of the United States Constitution. Individuals have the right to exercise their religion or choose not to follow any religion without interference or prejudice from the government. This includes the freedom to worship, pray, and practice religious rites, as well as the freedom to express religious views and viewpoints. Religious freedom is largely regarded as one of the most essential rights guaranteed by the Constitution and a foundation of American democracy. It is a fundamental aspect of religious liberty and a crucial feature in sustaining a varied and heterogeneous society.

Question 11: Which two rights are contained in the Declaration of Independence?

Explanation: Adopted by the Continental Congress on July 4, 1776, the Declaration of Independence announced the independence of the thirteen American colonies from British control and affirmed the rights of the American people. The Declaration of Independence does not give particular rights, but it does state "self-evident facts" on the structure of government and individual liberties. Two of the most well-known rights stated in the Declaration of Independence are:

- The Declaration says that all persons have an unalienable right to life, which means they have an inherent right to live and seek their own happiness.

- All individuals have an unalienable right to liberty, which implies they have the right to be free from oppressive or arbitrary government action, according to the Declaration of Independence.

Along with the right to property, these rights are widely regarded as the foundation of American political theory and continue to play an important role in American culture and democracy.

Question 12: What does "the rule of law" mean?

Explanation: All persons and organizations, along with the government, are accountable to and obligated by the law, according to the "rule of law" idea. It implies that everyone must adhere to the same rules, regardless of their status or authority, and that nobody is above the law. The rule of law is regarded as crucial for preserving individual rights and ensuring stability and justice in a democratic society. It guarantees that the law is implemented uniformly to all individuals and that government acts are constrained by legal limits and subject to judicial scrutiny. The rule of law is one of the defining characteristics of a democratic system and a crucial component in ensuring openness, accountability, and legal respect.

B: System of Government

Question 13: Who determines federal laws?

Explanation: In the United States, federal laws are created by the legislative part of the federal government, particularly the U.S. Congress. The two chambers of Congress are the House of Representatives and the Senate. A bill must be enacted by both the House of Representatives and the Senate and then signed into law by the President of the USA for it to become a federal law. If two-thirds of both the Senate and House of Representatives decide to override the President's veto, the measure can still become law. This method of lawmaking is outlined in the U.S. Constitution and is a fundamental part of the American government system and the separation of powers.

Question 14: What prevents a government branch from getting too powerful?

Explanation: The balance of power between the several components of the federal government prevents any one branch from being overly strong. This is known as the "separation of powers" and is a pillar of the American political system. Executive,

Legislative, and judicial are the three departments of the federal government, and each has distinct authorities and responsibilities.

Congress represents the legislative branch, which has the authority to pass laws. The President presides over the executive branch, which has the authority to implement laws and manage foreign policy. The Supreme Court, as well as other federal courts, represents the judicial branch, which has the authority to interpret laws and settle disputes.

This guarantees that each branch may verify and regulate the power of the others. The President can veto legislation enacted by Congress, but Congress can overturn vetoes with a two-thirds vote. The Supreme Court has the authority to declare legislation unlawful, so limiting the executive and legislative branches' authority.

This checks and balances system prevents any one arm of government from becoming excessively dominant, therefore fostering government stability, accountability, and the protection of citizen rights.

Question 15: Name one part or branch of the government.

Explanation: The U.S. government is organized into 3 branches, each with its own particular tasks and powers:

1. **Legislative Branch**: This branch is accountable for passing laws and is handled by the U.S. Congress, which

   comprises the House of Representatives and the Senate.

2. **Executive Branch**: This branch is accountable for law enforcement and is controlled by the President of the USA. The executive branch also comprises the Cabinet, the Vice President, and several federal agencies.

This branch is accountable for the interpretation of legislation and the resolution of disputes. It is governed by other federal courts and the Supreme Court.

Each one of these branches is an essential part of the U.S. government and operates together to preserve the checks and balances system that is at the core of the American democratic system.

Question 16: What two parts make up the US Congress?

Explanation: The legislative body of the federal government, the U.S. Congress, is responsible for enacting laws. It is comprised of the House of Representatives and the Senate.

The Senate is responsible for reviewing and approving presidential nominees for executive branch officials and federal judges and as well as legislative initiatives and treaties.

The House of Representatives is responsible for studying and approving legislation that impacts the American people. It has 435 members, each of whom represents a district within a state.

Before a bill may become law, it must be approved by both the House of Representatives and senate. The House of Representatives and the Senate collaborate to guarantee that the legislative arm of the federal government is responsible to the people it serves.

Question 17: Who is the current U.S. Senator from your state?

Explanation: Answers will vary. [Residents of the District of Columbia and U.S. territories should respond that D.C. (or the area in which they reside) has no U.S. Senators.

Question 18: For how many years do we elect a U.S. Senator?

Explanation: The term of a United States Senator is six years. This implies that once appointed, a Senator serves in the US Senate for six years before being eligible for re-election or replacement.

Question 19: How many United States Senators exist?

Explanation: There are 100 Senators in total in the US Congress. The Senate is one of the two chambers of the US Congress, with the House of Representatives being the other. Each state, regardless of its population or size, is represented by 2 Senators who serve in the Senate to reflect the interests of their voters and contribute to the making of national laws.

Question 20: Please provide the name of your United States Representative.

Explanation: The U.S. Representative is the individual elected to represent the residents of a given congressional district in the House of Representatives. You may find out who your U.S. Representative is by visiting the House of Representatives official website, contacting your local election office, or contacting your state's Secretary of State. In addition, you may visit the official websites of political parties and utilize internet tools like voting and government websites.

Question 21: How many years do we elect a U.S. Representative to serve?

Explanation: A Representative of the United States is elected for a two-year term. This implies that once elected, a Representative works in the House of Representatives for 2 years before being eligible for reelection or replacement. The two-year tenure for Representatives permits frequent elections and enables constituents to hold their Representatives responsible. This system ensures that the people's interests are adequately reflected in the legislative arm of the federal government.

Question 22: How many members of the House of Representatives are eligible to vote?

Explanation: There are 435 voting representatives in the House of Representatives. In 1911, Congress approved a statute setting the number of representatives in the House at 435. The no. of Representatives a state has is proportional to its population, with each state guaranteed at least one. Every 10 years following the census, the number of Representatives from each state is recalculated to ensure that each state's population is adequately represented in the House.

Question 23: Who do United States Senators represent?

Explanation: Senators represent the full population of the state they were elected to represent. Each state has 2 Senators who serve in the US Senate to represent the concerns of their citizens and contribute to the drafting of national legislation. Senators are elected to serve the interests of all state residents, regardless of their political opinions or connections. This implies that Senators are obligated to consider the requirements and opinions of all of their constituents and to make choices that are in their constituents' best interests as a whole.

Question 24: Who is the President of the United States currently?

Explanation: Joe Biden was inaugurated as President of the United States on January 20, 2021. It is essential to highlight that the President of the United States is elected for a four-year term and is eligible for re-election.

Question 25: What month is the election for President held?

Explanation: In the United States, the presidential election is traditionally held on the Tuesday after the first Monday of November. Every four years, residents from around the United States vote in this election to select who will serve as the following President of the United States. Citizens elect the President of the United States using an electoral college system, meaning that the victor of the election is chosen by the result of the electoral college votes rather than the popular vote. Elections are held in November to guarantee that the President-elect has sufficient time to prepare for their transition into the office prior to their inauguration in January of the following year.

Question 26: Presidents are elected for how many years?

Explanation: The President of the USA is chosen for a four-year term. This implies that once appointed, a President serves as the head of the executive arm of the federal government for four years, after which they may seek reelection or be replaced by a new President. The President's four-year term allows for a continuous election cycle and ensures that the President is responsible to the American people. In addition, the President can be re-elected for a second, identically four-year term.

However, the 22nd Amendment to the United States Constitution restricts a President to a maximum of two terms in office.

Question 27: Why do certain states have a larger number of Representatives than others?

Explanation: Population determines the number of Representatives a state has in the House of Representatives. Each state must be represented in the House of Representatives, and the number of Representatives a state has depends on its population, with each state promised at least one Representative under the Constitution. This indicates that states with greater populations have more House Representatives than those with lower populations. Every 10 years following the census, the number of Representatives from each state is recalculated to ensure that each state's population is adequately represented in the House.

This form of representation ensures that each state has an equal say in the legislative process and that the people's interests are adequately reflected in the federal government. The principle behind this system is that each person's vote must carry about the same value, regardless of where they live, and that a state's number of Representatives should correspond to its population.

Question 28: What is the current name of the United States Vice President?

Explanation: Kamala Harris became the Vice President of the United States on January 20, 2021. Notably, the Vice President of the United States is elected alongside the President and acts as the President of the Senate and a cabinet member. In the case that the President is unable to carry out their duties, the Vice President is the next in line to assume the presidency. Additionally, the Vice President may be allocated additional tasks by the President.

Question 29: Who succeeds the President if he is unable to serve?

Explanation: If the US president is unable to execute their responsibilities or is no longer able to serve, the Vice President becomes the President. This is stipulated under the Presidential Succession Act of 1947's succession line. In the case that the President is unable to carry out their duties, the line of succession defines the order in which federal government officials will assume the presidency.

It is essential to have a clear succession plan in place to safeguard the stability and continuation of the administration in the event that the president becomes incapacitated. This guarantees that there is a clear path for the transfer of power to a new President and helps to eliminate uncertainty and power voids in the aftermath of a presidential vacancy.

Question 30: Who designates bills as laws?

Explanation: For a bill to become law in the United States, it must go through a number of stages and be approved by both the Senate and the House of Representatives, as well as the President. A measure has to be submitted to the House and then approved by the Senate before it can become law. After a measure passes both houses of Congress, it goes to the President of the United States for confirmation.

The President can give the measure his "executive approval" and make it law. If the President signs the measure into law, it receives a public law number and enters into force. If the President doesn't want to sign the measure into law, he can veto it instead, making it ineffective until it's overcome by a two-thirds majority of votes in both chambers of Congress. The measure will become law without the President's approval if he or she does not sign it within 10 days (not counting Sundays) of getting it from Congress.

After measures have passed through both chambers of Congress, the President signs them into law. The President's signature on a bill is a crucial part of the legislative process since it shows that the President supports the measure.

Question 31: Who is the chief commander of the military?

Explanation: President of the United States holds the position of Commander in Chief of the United States military.

The President of the United States is the nation's highest-ranking military leader, and as such, he or she is ultimately responsible for the strategic and operational oversight of the armed forces. The Constitution of the USA designates the President as Commander in Chief, giving him or her command of the armed forces during war and peace.

The President is the head of the military, with the authority to make decisions on the use of force and to direct the actions of the military. The President also chooses the

Secretary of Defense and other senior military officers and guides the military's general policy and direction.

In addition to leading the armed forces, the President also has the authority to make policy choices on the military's structure and composition and to issue pardons and amnesty for serving members. An integral part of the President's job is to lead the armed forces in protecting the country and its population.

Question 32: What happens if neither the President nor the Vice President can continue in office?

Explanation: If both the Vice President and President of the United States are incapacitated at the same time, the Speaker of the House of Representatives automatically assumes the presidency. After the Vice President, the Speaker of the House is next in line to become President. In the event that both the Vice President and President are unable to serve in their positions, the Presidential Succession Act of 1947 establishes the sequence of succession to the presidency.

Others in the federal government's highest ranks are also included in the line of succession. These include the Senate's President pro tempore, the Secretary of State and other members of the Cabinet. If the House Speaker is unable to fulfill his or her duties, the Senate's President pro tempore will take over, then the Secretary of State, and so on.

If the Vice President and President are both unable to serve, it is crucial to have a defined line of succession in place to maintain the continuation and stability of the administration. This facilitates a smooth transition of power from the outgoing to the incoming President by eliminating any potential for ambiguity or voids in authority.

Question 33: Who has the authority to veto bills?

Explanation: The President of the USA has the authority to veto legislation enacted by both houses of Congress (the Senate and the House of Representatives). For the President to reject a measure and keep it from becoming law, he or she must use a veto.

Ten days (not including Sundays) are given to the President to sign or reject a measure after it is delivered to him or her. Upon the President's signature, the measure enters into force. If the

President vetoes a measure, the bill and an explanation of the veto's reasoning are sent back to the chamber from whence it came.

A veto from the President requires a two-thirds majority vote from each chamber of Congress to overturn. To pass, a law needs the support of a majority of senators (67 of 100) and a majority of representatives (290 of 435) in both houses of Congress. If the measure passes both houses of Congress over the President's veto, it becomes law.

A Presidential veto is a powerful tool that ensures the President's priorities are taken into account during the lawmaking process. It also aids in keeping the legislative and executive parts of government in check with one another.

Question 34: What is the United States' highest court?

Explanation: The United State's highest court is the Supreme Court. The Supreme Court has the authority to construe the Constitution and make judgments that are obligatory on all other courts in the nation.

Nine justices are selected by the President and approved by the Senate to compose the Supreme Court. A judicial is appointed for life or till they resign or retire. The Chief Justice of the Supreme Court takes precedence over the Court and oversees its operations.

The Supreme Court has the authority to examine cases involving significant issues of federal law, especially challenges to the legitimacy of federal legislation or executive actions. In addition, the Supreme Court has exclusive jurisdiction over a subset of issues, such as conflicts between 2 or more states.

The rulings of the United States Supreme Court are among the most significant and influential judicial decisions in the country. The decisions of the Supreme Court have a tremendous impact on American culture and frequently establish legal precedents that determine future court decisions and the evolution of the law.

Question 35: What is the role of the judicial branch?

Explanation: In one of the three departments of the federal government of the US, the judicial branch is responsible for interpreting and enforcing the law.

It is the responsibility of the judicial branch to interpret the Constitution and federal laws, and it has the authority to hear and consider matters involving these laws. This covers disputes between individuals, organizations, states, the federal government, and foreign nations.

The federal judiciary consists of a court hierarchy, with the Supreme Court serving as the nation's highest court. The federal court system also consists of the Courts of Appeals, which review appeals from the district courts, and the lower District Courts, which serve as the federal system's trial courts and handle disputes concerning federal law.

In addition to interpreting and implementing the law, the judicial branch plays a crucial role in preserving the delicate power balance among the three departments of government. By hearing cases that question the conduct of the legislative and executive departments, the judiciary serves to guarantee that the federal government functions within the Constitution and national laws.

Question 36: What are a couple of high-ranking positions in the Cabinet?

Explanation: In the United States, the Cabinet is comprised of the Vice President and the leaders of 15 executive departments. These departments, referred to as Cabinet-level positions, act as the chief advisors to the President and play a crucial role in the effective operation of the federal government. Here are two examples of Cabinet-level positions:

1. The Secretary of State: Responsible for the management of foreign policy, representing the US abroad, and providing the President with key advice on international affairs.

2. The Secretary of the Treasury: Overseeing the nation's finances, including currency and coin production, tax collection, and government debt management. This position also serves as the President's primary economic advisor. These are only a couple of examples of Cabinet-level positions. Other

executive departments include the Department of Defense, the Department of Justice, and the Department of Homeland Security, among many others. Each department has its own distinct responsibilities and contributes to implementing the President's policies and serving the needs of the American people.

Question 37: How does the President's Cabinet operate?

Explanation: The President's Cabinet is composed of the highest-ranking officials appointed to the executive branch of the federal government of the United States, including the Vice President and the leaders of 15 executive departments. The Cabinet serves as the primary advisory group to the President and is responsible for providing counsel on policy and administrative matters, as well as aiding the President in making informed decisions. Cabinet members often offer their expertise on complicated issues and help develop policies and programs that benefit the American people.

In addition to advising the President, the Cabinet has a critical role in the day-to-day operation of the federal government. Cabinet members are in charge of overseeing their departments and serving as primary representatives, communicating the President's policies to the American people, and collaborating with Congress to advance the President's legislative agenda. Ultimately, the Cabinet plays an essential role in guiding the direction of the federal government, ensuring that the executive branch functions efficiently and effectively in serving the needs of the American people.

Question 38: What is the number of justices in the Supreme Court?

Explanation: The United States Supreme Court is the highest court in the federal judiciary system, consisting of nine justices appointed by the President and confirmed by the Senate. Members include the Supreme Court's Chief Justice and eight other associate justices. As the final interpreters of the law, the justices determine cases and interpret the Constitution. The decisions they make can have significant impacts on American society, highlighting the court's crucial role as one of the most important institutions in the country.

Question 39: What is the length of service for a U.S. Senator?

Explanation: The term of service for a U.S. Senator is 6 years. Upon election, a senator serves a 6-year term before being required to seek re-election. To maintain stability and continuity in the Senate, the terms of senators are staggered so that only roughly one-third of the Senate faces re-election at a given time. This approach encourages long-term planning and decision-making by senators.

Question 40: What is the current name of the Speaker of the House of Representatives?

Explanation: At present, the Speaker of the House of Representatives is Kevin McCarthy, a member of the Republican Party. The House of Representatives elects the Speaker, and their tenure lasts for two years, coinciding with the beginning of each new Congress. To obtain the most current information, it is best to consult a reliable government website or recent news reports.

Question 41: Who is the current Governor of your state?

Explanation: To find out the name of the current governor of your state, you can check a reliable news source or the official website of your state government.

Question 42: What is the current political party of the President?

Explanation: At present, the President belongs to the Democratic Party. Political affiliations can shift over time, and to obtain the most accurate information, it is recommended to consult a trustworthy news source or government website.

Question 43: What are America's two major political parties?

Explanation: In the United States, the two largest political parties are the Republican Party and the Democratic Party. In general, the Democratic Party is viewed as more liberal and progressive, whereas the Republican Party is viewed as a more conservative and pro-limited government. These generalizations are not usually accurate, as many members of each party have a wide variety of political opinions and ideals.

Question 44: What is your state's capital?

Explanation: For the purpose of the U.S. citizenship test, you would be required to identify the capital of the state in which you reside. For example, if you reside in California, Sacramento is the capital. If you reside in New York, the state capital is Albany.

Question 45: Our Constitution grants the states certain authority. What is one of the state's powers?

Explanation: Some powers are kept for the states under the U.S. Constitution, meaning they are not delegated entirely to the federal government. This notion, known as federalism, is meant to strike a balance between the states and the federal government.

Among the several instances of state powers are the capacity to:

1. Control commerce inside the state

2. Govern and license occupations

3. Regulate elections and voting processes

4. Adopt changes to the United States Constitution

5. Control natural resources within the bounds of the state.

This is not an entire list, but these are a few instances of the powers granted to the states under the United States Constitution.

Question 46: Our Constitution grants the federal government certain authorities. What is one of the federal government's powers?

Explanation: According to the US Constitution, the federal government has defined, delineated authorities, often known as enumerated powers. They include the ability to regulate interstate trade, create currency, declare war, and regulate immigration. The purpose of granting these powers to the federal government was to create a powerful central government that could efficiently rule the country as a whole while protecting the sovereignty of the various states.

Question 47: Who is the United States' current Chief Justice?

Explanation: The Chief Justice of the United States presides over the Supreme Court. John Roberts is the present Chief Justice of the United States. He has held this office since 2005.

C: Rights and Responsibilities

Question 48: Identify a privilege exclusive to United States citizens.

Explanation: Some rights and advantages are reserved solely for United States citizens. Voting in federal elections, running for federal office, working for the federal government, and petitioning for specific family members to move to the United States are all examples of these privileges. In addition to being secured by the Constitution and Laws of this Country, including the Bill of Rights, U.S. citizens can get consular aid when overseas.

Question 49: What are two rights that every American citizen has?

Explanation: The First Amendment to the United States Constitution guarantees the freedom of speech and religion to all citizens. This implies that every person in the United States has the freedom to openly express their views, beliefs, and opinions, as well as to practice their religion without governmental interference. These rights are deemed basic and are guaranteed by the law, allowing individuals to freely practice their opinions and engage in public conversation without fear of reprisal.

Question 50: What is a duty that only United States citizens must fulfill?

Explanation: Voting in federal elections is a task that only United States citizens are required to fulfill. Only citizens are entitled to vote in congressional, presidential, and other elections, and exercising this privilege and participating in the political process is considered a civic obligation. Additional obligations of citizenship include serving on a jury if summoned, paying taxes, and abiding by the country's rules and regulations.

Question 51: Regarding eligibility to vote, the Constitution has four amendments. Specify one of these.

Explanation: The 15th Amendment, passed in 1870, is one of the 4 amendments to the Constitution regarding eligibility to vote. This amendment specifies that the right to vote will not be denied or restricted on the basis of race, color, or past condition of slavery by the United States or any state. In other words, the 15th Amendment ensures the right to vote for all people, regardless of race or color.

Question 52: When we say the Pledge of Allegiance, we demonstrate allegiance to what?

Explanation: The Pledge of Allegiance is an affirmation of allegiance and devotion to the United States of America and its founding ideals. While saying the Pledge of Allegiance, one pledges loyalty to the American flag and the Republic for which it stands: one country under God, undivided, with justice and freedom for all. The Pledge of Allegiance is typically repeated in public schools and other patriotic occasions and is frequently viewed as a means of expressing one's love and respect for one's nation.

Question 53: When you become a U.S. citizen, what is one pledge you make?

Explanation: When you become a citizen of the United States, you pledge to defend and support the laws and Constitution of the United States, to retain true faith and loyalty to them, and to relinquish any foreign loyalties and/or foreign titles. This pledge is known as the Oath of Allegiance, and it is an essential component of the citizenship process. By taking the Oath, you pledge allegiance to the United States and its democratic ideals and values.

Question 54: When are all males required to register with the Selective Service?

All male immigrants and male U.S. citizens between the ages of 18 and 25 are obliged to register with the Selective Service System. The registration requirement reflects the government's desire to keep an accurate list of possible military recruits in the case of a national disaster necessitating a military draught. The

Selective Service System would then utilize the registration data to select persons for military duty.

Question 55: When is the deadline for filing federal income tax returns?

Explanation: The annual deadline for filing federal income tax returns in the United States is April 15. Individuals must submit their federal income tax returns by this date or seek an extension. If an extension is permitted, the due date for filing the tax return is typically extended to October 15th. But, the delay does not affect the deadline for paying any outstanding taxes. It is crucial to note that this date may vary owing to holidays or other situations; thus, it is recommended to consult the Internal Revenue Service's (IRS) website for the most current information.

Question 56: How can Americans engage in their democracy in two ways?

Explanation: There are several ways for Americans to engage in their democracy, including:

- Voting in elections is one of the essential methods to engage in a democracy. Voting allows citizens to pick their leaders and influence the destiny of the nation.

- Forming a political party is also another means through which Americans can engage in their democracy. Citizens can advocate for their opinions and support politicians who share those values through political parties.

- Engaging in Campaigns: People may also engage in campaigns by contributing their resources and time to support a candidate or by volunteering their time and resources.

- Contacting Elected Authorities Another option to participate in democracy is to engage elected officials through letters, phone calls, or personal visits to their offices. This enables individuals to voice their opinions on significant issues and push for policies they favor.

- People can also assist in democracy by joining advocacy groups that aim to advance particular topics or problems. These organizations provide a forum for residents to share their opinions on subjects that are significant to them.

Question 57: What age must citizens be to vote for President?

Explanation: A citizen must be at least 18 years old in order to vote for president in the United States. The voting age in the United States is from 21 to 18 according to the 26th Amendment.

3.2 American History

A: Colonial Period and Independence

Question 58: Who inhabited America before the arrival of Europeans?

Explanation: Before the advent of Europeans, indigenous peoples, sometimes known as Native Americans, inhabited North America. The culture, history, and customs of these tribes were distinct to each tribe and location. The indigenous peoples of the United States have a rich and diversified heritage that dates back thousands of years, and they've played a significant role in American history since its inception.

Question 59: Why did certain colonists come to America?

Explanation: There are several reasons why colonists arrived in America. Among the most frequent causes are:

Many colonists immigrated to America to escape religious persecution in Europe and to freely practice their religion.

The colonies provided economic prospects and the opportunity to begin a new life with resources and land.

Some colonists wanted political independence and political freedom from European domination.

Several colonists came to the United States as adventurers and to investigate the new world.

Some people were taken to America as enslaved Africans or indentured servants and had no option but to go to the United States.

Each group of colonists had its own motives and reasons for emigrating to the United States, but the following are some of the most prevalent explanations.

Question 60: Which group was brought to America and sold as slaves?

Explanation: This question pertains to the historical context of slavery in the US. Africans were brought to the United States and sold as slaves. Slavery was a system in which individuals were purchased and sold as property and compelled to work for free. It endured for more than 200 years, until the end of the Civil War and the enactment of the 13th Amendment to the Constitution, which ended slavery in the United States.

Question 61: There were 13 original states. Name three.

Explanation: The 13 original states in the United States are:

1. Pennsylvania
2. Delaware
3. New Jersey
4. Connecticut
5. Georgia
6. Rhode Island
7. Massachusetts
8. South Carolina
9. Maryland
10. New Hampshire
11. New York
12. Virginia
13. North Carolina

Question 62: When did the Independence Declaration become official?

Explanation: On July 4, 1776, the Independence Declaration was adopted. The Declaration of Independence is a document that asserts the freedom of the thirteen American colonies from the British Empire and serves as the basis for the United States of America. Thomas Jefferson authored the Declaration, which was accepted by the Continental Congress, the regulatory authority of the colonies at the time. The Declaration of Independence has become an iconic emblem of American freedom and democracy, and Independence Day is still observed yearly on July 4.

Question 63: Who is the author of the Independence Declaration?

Explanation: Thomas Jefferson authored the Declaration of Independence. He was a founding father of the United States whose writings and political theory were well-known. On July 4, 1776, the Continental Congress approved the Declaration of Independence, which declared the split of the 13 American colonies from Great Britain. The manifesto describes the colonies' grievances against the British authority and asserts their right to autonomy. It is regarded as the foundation of American democracy and continues to be one of the most significant papers in American history.

Question 64: Why did the colonists wage war against the British?

Explanation: The colonists fought the British in the American Revolutionary War (1775-1783) because they thought they were being treated unfairly and that their rights were being infringed by the British government. The colonists were enraged over a variety of matters, including:

The British government was taxing the colonists without their approval, which the colonists claimed violated their privileges as British citizens.

Limitations on commerce The British government restricted the economic potential of the colonists by restricting trade with the colonies.

The British government required colonists to provide lodging for British soldiers, which the colonists perceived as an infringement of their rights.

The British government was attempting to assert more authority over the colonial administrations, which the colonists perceived as a danger to their independence.

The colonists thought that the British government's acts were wrong and that they were obligated to fight for their freedom and liberty. This resulted in the American Revolutionary War, which ultimately led to the establishment of the United States of America.

Question 65: What transpired during the Convention on the Constitution?

Explanation: In 1787, delegates from the 13 American states gathered in Philadelphia, Pennsylvania, for the Constitutional Convention. The goal of the conference was to amend the Articles of Confederation, the first constitution of the United States, which many founding fathers deemed insufficient. Nonetheless, the Constitutional Convention produced a totally new constitution, which has since become the ultimate law of the state.

At the Constitutional Convention, 55 state representatives convened to discuss and debate the nation's destiny. A number of significant issues were discussed, including the division of power between the federal government and the states, the form of the legislative and executive departments of government, and the preservation of individual rights. The Constitution was signed by the delegates on September 17, 1787, following several months of heated debate and negotiations.

The result of the Constitutional Convention was the establishment of a new system of government that strikes a balance between the federal and state governments, preserves individual liberties, and provides for the common defense and general welfare of the people. The Constitution has been revised 27 times throughout the centuries, but its fundamental structure and concepts have remained the same, making it the world's oldest written national constitution currently in operation.

Question 66: What is one item for which Benjamin Franklin is known?

Explanation: Benjamin Franklin was a polymath who was renowned for his accomplishments. This is something he is well-known for:

Benjamin Franklin's work with electricity, particularly the famous kite test in which he established that lightning is a kind of electricity, has made him renowned. Moreover, he designed the lightning rod that was employed to protect structures from lightning strikes. His investigations contributed to the contemporary knowledge of electricity and gave him a distinction as one of the most distinguished scientists of his day.

Benjamin Franklin was not just a scientist but also a publisher, author, statesman, and diplomat. He was one of the United States' founding fathers and played a significant role in the American Revolution. He also was a delegate to the Continental Congress and the governor of Pennsylvania, in addition to signing the Declaration of Independence and the United States Constitution. He is regarded as one of the most significant personalities in the history of the United States.

Question 67: The Federalist Papers advocated for the adoption of the United States Constitution. Mention one of the authors.

Explanation: Alexander Hamilton, James Madison, and John Jay wrote the Federalist Papers to advocate for the adoption of the United States Constitution. These articles, which were issued in 1787 and 1788 in several publications, presented an in-depth study of the Constitution and described the reasoning behind its provisions.

Alexander Hamilton was one of the Federalist Papers three writers. He was one of the country's first Secretaries of the Treasury and a founding father of the United States. He was a significant contributor to the growth of the American economy and a staunch supporter of a solid federal government.

James Madison contributed to the writing of the Federalist Papers. He was one of the principal architects of the Constitution and a founding father of the United States. He is also regarded as the "Father of the Constitution" and was the 4th President of the United States.

The 3rd author of the Founding Documents was John Jay. He served as the country's first Chief Judge of the Supreme Court and was a founding father of the United States. He was an ardent advocate of the Constitution and was instrumental in its approval.

The Federalist Papers are frequently read and studied by historians and scholars of American government and history because they continue to be recognized as a key source of insight into the ideas and reasoning underlying the United States Constitution.

Question 68: When was the United States Constitution written?

Explanation: The Constitution of the United States was drafted in 1787. The Constitutional Convention was held in Philadelphia, Pennsylvania, from May 25 to September 17, 1787, with delegates from thirteen states in attendance. At this convention, the participants talked and debated the nation's future and the appropriate form of governance. Following several months of heated deliberations, the delegates decided on the language of the Constitution, which was signed on September 17, 1787, by 39 of the 55 delegates.

The Constitution was subsequently presented to the states for approval, and New Hampshire became the 9th state to approve it on June 21, 1788. Since being the highest law of the state, the Constitution has been modified 27 times over the ages. It is the world's oldest written national constitution, still in effect today.

Question 69: Who was the 1st President of the United States?

Explanation: George Washington served as the first President of the United States. In 1788, he was chosen as the nation's first president, and he assumed office on April 30, 1789. Washington served as president for two terms, from 1789 to 1797, and was crucial in creating many of the rituals and traditions now associated with the office.

Washington was a prominent player in the American Revolution and a military hero. He played a crucial part in the Continental Army's triumph over the British and was highly regarded for his honesty and leadership. In addition to being a member of the Constitutional Convention, where he was one of the people who signed the United States Constitution, he was also a signatory.

As president, George Washington fought to set up a new federal government and create a powerful, cohesive nation. He fought to establish the power of the presidency and the other institutions of government and was a staunch supporter of a strong federal government. He was also instrumental in developing strong ties with other nations, especially the United Kingdom, and building the groundwork for a stable and successful nation.

George Washington is largely recognized as one of the finest presidents in American history, and he continues to serve as a significant symbol of American freedom and democracy.

Question 70: Who is referred to as the "Father of Our Country"?

Explanation: The term "Father of Our Nation" is frequently applied in reference to George Washington, the nation's first president. Washington is commonly referred to as the "Father of Our Nation" in honor of his numerous contributions to the founding and prosperity of the United States.

Washington was a prominent player in the American Revolution and a military hero. He played a pivotal part in the Continental Army's triumph over the British, and he was universally admired for his honesty and leadership. In addition to being a participant in the Constitutional Convention, where he was among the signers of the United States Constitution, he was also a signatory.

As the first US president, George Washington was instrumental in establishing the federal government and constructing a powerful, unified country. He fought to establish the power of the presidency and the other institutions of government and was a staunch supporter of a strong federal government. He was also instrumental in developing strong ties with other nations, especially the United Kingdom, and building the groundwork for a stable and successful nation.

George Washington is largely recognized as one of the finest presidents in American history, and he continues to serve as a significant symbol of American freedom and democracy. The moniker "Father of Our Nation" reflects the profound regard and affection many Americans have for George Washington and his accomplishments for the nation.

B: 1800's

Question 71: Provide the name of the North-South war in the United States.

Explanation: The fight between the North and South of the United States is often referred to as the American Civil War. From 1861-65, it was fought mostly over slavery and state rights. Growing tensions existed at the time between the Northern states, which were mostly industrialized and had limited use for enslavement, and the Southern states, whose agricultural economy relied heavily on slavery.

The American Civil War was among the most destructive conflicts in American history, resulting in the loss of hundreds of thousands of people and enormous property destruction. Notwithstanding its brutality, the Civil War is usually seen as a key point in American history, as it led to the abolition of slavery and the survival of the Union.

The American Civil War continues to be one of the most researched and debated events in American history, and historians and researchers continue to argue its origins and effects at length. Regardless of one's opinion, it is universally acknowledged as a defining moment in American history, and it continues to affect the social and political landscape of the country to this day.

Question 72: Name one war waged by the U. S. in the nineteenth century.

Explanation: The Mexican-American War, which lasted from 1846 to 1848, was one of the wars waged by the United States in the nineteenth century. The conflict between the USA and Mexico was precipitated by American expansionism and a disagreement over the boundary between Texas, which the United States had recently acquired, and Mexico.

The Mexican-American War was an important event in American history because it resulted in the acquisition of a vast amount of additional territory, along with what are now the states of Nevada, California, Utah, New Mexico, Arizona, and Colorado, as well as portions of Wyoming, Oklahoma, Texas, Kansas, and Colorado. The conflict also helped establish the United States as a major force in the Western Hemisphere and marked the start of the United States ascent as a significant international power.

Many Americans opposed the expansionist goals of the government and the concept of war with a neighboring nation, notwithstanding the importance of the Mexican-American War. The conflict had long-lasting effects on the relationship between Mexico and the United States, and it is still an important occurrence in the histories of both nations.

Question 73: In 1803, what land did the U. S. purchase from France?

Explanation: In 1803, the United States acquired from France a massive stretch of territory known as the Louisiana Purchase. This region encompassed more than 800,000 square miles and comprised portions of 15 states, including Missouri, Arkansas, Iowa, South Dakota, North Dakota, Nebraska, Louisiana, Oklahoma, Kansas, Texas, Montana, Colorado, Wyoming, and portions of Minnesota, among others.

The Louisiana Purchase marked a significant extension of American territory and was one of the greatest land purchases in American history. It was motivated by the desire to obtain more territory for westward development and to defend American interests in the region's expanding trade and commerce.

The Louisiana Purchase represented America's first major push into foreign diplomacy and territory expansion. The agreement with France was viewed as a tremendous accomplishment for President Thomas Jefferson, who played a crucial role in negotiating the purchase conditions.

The Louisiana Purchase was a significant point in American history because it set the door for westward expansion and helped establish the United States as a dominant power in the Western Hemisphere.

Question 74: Identify one issue that contributed to the Civil War.

Explanation: Slavery contributed to the onset of the American Civil War. Slavery had been a divisive topic in the United States since its inception, and hostilities between Northern states, which primarily opposed slavery, and Southern ones, which relied significantly on slavery for their agricultural economy, approached a flash point in the decades preceding the Civil War.

As the country continued to grow and more areas were added, the subject of whether enslavement would be permitted in these new states grew more problematic. This topic was at the center of the sectional tensions that eventually led to the Civil War.

The Southern states, believing that the federal government was infringing upon their sovereignty, seceded from the Union and founded the Confederate States of America.

The Northern states, which believed in maintaining the Union and abolishing slavery, replied by declaring war.

Other issues, such as economic divisions, cultural and social divides, and divergent perspectives on the function of the federal government, also contributed to the Civil War. Regardless of the causes, the American Civil War continues to be one of the most destructive and transformational events in American history, and its influence continues to affect the nation.

Question 75: What was done by Susan B. Anthony?

Explanation: Susan B. Anthony was a renowned American activist and social reformer who was instrumental in the movement for women's rights. She was born in Massachusetts in 1820 and raised in a household devoted to social equality and the eradication of slavery.

Anthony was an ardent supporter of women's suffrage and rights, or the right of women to vote, throughout her life. She was a prominent member of the National Woman Suffrage Association, a group that fought for women's right to vote, and she traveled the country making speeches and organizing rallies and protests in support of the cause.

Anthony was also active in other movements for social change, such as temperance (the struggle to prohibit alcohol), workers' liberties, and abolition. Her relentless advocacy for equality and justice inspired numerous more to join the struggle for women's rights.

Susan B. Anthony remains one of the most influential personalities in American history, as her legacy continues to motivate others to this day. Her contributions laid the groundwork for the current women's rights movement, and she is largely viewed as a pioneer and a champion for women's rights.

Question 76: What was the role of the Emancipation Proclamation?

Explanation: The Emancipation Proclamation was an executive order and presidential proclamation issued by Abraham Lincoln on January 1, 1863, during the

American Civil War. Its objective was to declare all slaves in Southern territory free and to undermine the Confederacy by removing its primary source of labor.

The Emancipation Proclamation only extended to slaves in territory held by the Confederacy and did not immediately release a single slave. Yet, it had a profound effect on the Civil War and the destiny of the nation. The Emancipation Proclamation shifted the focus of the Civil War from maintaining the Union to eradicating slavery, paving the way for the 13th Amendment, which ended slavery in the country.

In conclusion, the Emancipation Proclamation was a crucial step in the elimination of slavery in the USA and continues to be a significant symbol of freedom and equality.

Question 77: What was the most significant thing Abraham Lincoln did?

Explanation: Serving as the 16th President of the USA during a period of immense national crisis was one of Abraham Lincoln's most significant accomplishments. Throughout the American Civil War, Lincoln led the nation through one of its darkest eras.

The Union was capable of defeating the Confederate and retaining the US as a single, cohesive nation under the leadership of Abraham Lincoln. The country was galvanized by Lincoln's addresses, such as the Gettysburg Address, which mobilized support for the war effort. In 1863, he also released the Emancipation Proclamation, which liberated slaves in Confederate-controlled territory and set the stage for the ultimate elimination of slavery in the country.

Lincoln is largely regarded as one of the greatest American presidents and is remembered for his honesty, determination to preserve the Union, and efforts to abolish slavery. His leadership throughout the American Civil War influenced the

trajectory of American history, and his legacy remains an inspiration to people all around the world.

C: Recent American History and Other Important Historical Information

Question 78: Who led the United States during World War I?

Explanation: Woodrow Wilson was the President of the USA during World War I. From 1913 through 1921, he was President for two terms.

Wilson was president in 1917 when the US entered World War I. He was a staunch supporter of US participation in the war, claiming that it was important to safeguard American interests and promote freedom and democracy worldwide. Wilson played a vital influence in creating American foreign policy and directing the nation through one of the most serious international crises during his administration.

Wilson was a significant actor in the international attempt to achieve permanent peace after the war, and he was instrumental in negotiating the conditions of the Treaty of Versailles, which formally ended the war. His "14 Points" speech, which outlined a goal for a world of cooperation and peace and his promotion of the League of Nations, a precursor to the United Nations, is his most enduring legacies.

Ultimately, Woodrow Wilson was a significant character in American history, and his leadership during World War I had a profound effect on the nation and the world.

Question 79: In the 1900s, the United States fought one war.

Explanation: The United States participated in World War I, often referred to as the Great War, during the 20th century. The war continued from 1914 to 1918 and was a worldwide struggle involving the main nations of the world. In 1917, the United States joined the war on behalf of the Allies (comprised of Britain, France, and Russia) and played a crucial role in assisting in overthrowing the Central Powers.

The multifaceted roots of World War I comprised economic, political, and military elements. The conflict had a tremendous effect on the world, resulting in massive changes to political boundaries, the emergence of new countries, and the demise of existing empires. The war resulted in tremendous economic development in the United States, a shift in the country's position in international affairs, and a greater emphasis on military preparation and national security.

Ultimately, World War I was an important matter in the history of the USA and the globe, and it remains crucial to study and comprehend to this day.

Question 80: Who served as the nation's chief executive throughout the Great Depression and World War II?

Explanation: Franklin D. Roosevelt was the President of the USA during World War I and Great Depression I, serving an extraordinary four terms from 1933 to 1945.

Roosevelt assumed the presidency during the Great Depression, which lasted from 1929 until the late 1930s and was a severe economic disaster. He started a series of initiatives and reforms together, known as the New Deal, intended to provide unemployment relief, stabilize the economy, and foster economic recovery.

Roosevelt originally tried to maintain American neutrality when World War II erupted in Europe in 1939, but he ultimately judged that American action was vital to defeat the Axis forces (led by Japan, Germany, and Italy). He gave essential assistance to the Allies (headed by the United Kingdom and the Soviet Union) and assisted in galvanizing public opinion in support of the war effort.

As the United States joined the war in 1941, Roosevelt was instrumental in defining American policy and directing the worldwide campaign to defeat the Axis forces. In addition, he collaborated closely with Allied powers, notably Winston Churchill and Joseph Stalin, to organize and execute the war effort.

Ultimately, Franklin D. Roosevelt was among the most influential presidents in American history, and his presidency throughout the Great Depression and World War II left an indelible mark on the nation and the globe.

Question 81: Provide the name of one American Indian tribe.

Explanation: The Navajo Nation is one of the American Indian tribes in the United States. The Navajo are the most populous Native American tribe in the United States, and their reservation is situated in the 4 Corners region of the American Southwest, which includes portions of New Mexico, Arizona, and Utah.

The Navajo have a profound relationship with the land and a rich cultural history. They have a long and illustrious history, stretching back hundreds of years, and have persisted despite decades of obstacles, including forced marches and relocation from their original lands, and tried to incorporate them into American mainstream culture.

Today, the Navajo Nation is a prosperous, self-governing nation of more than 300,000 individuals. The Navajo language is extensively spoken, and Navajo culture remains an essential component of the tribe's heritage. The Navajo have played a crucial part in defining the culture and history of the southwestern United States and have made substantial contributions to American society.

Ultimately, the Navajo represent a significant component of America's rich cultural legacy, and their achievements and customs remain a fundamental element of contemporary American society.

Question 82: What big event occurred in the United States on September 11, 2001?

Explanation: Terrorist attacks on the Pentagon in Washington, D.C., and the World Trade Center in New York City were the main events of September 11, 2001, in the United States.

On that fatal day, terrorists affiliated with the extremist organization Al-Qaeda seized four passenger airliners. 2 of the airplanes crashed into the World Trade Center's Twin Towers in New York City, resulting in the towers' collapse and the deaths of almost 3,000 people. Another jet was driven into the Pentagon in Washington, D.C., resulting in the deaths of more than 100 individuals. United Airlines Flight 93 was on its route to a target in Washington, D.C., but the crew and passengers attempted to regain control of the aircraft before it fell into a field in Pennsylvania, killing everybody aboard.

The terrorist attacks on September 11, 2001, were a catastrophe for the United States and the whole globe. These resulted in a significant shift in American international and domestic policy, including the commencement of the "War on Terror" and the invasion of Afghanistan, in addition to heightened measures to strengthen national security and information collecting.

The tragedies of September 11, 2001, remain an important and sad turning point in American history and serve as a potent reminder of the significance of vigilance and security in the modern world.

Question 83: What actions did Martin Luther King Jr. take?

Explanation: American Baptist clergyman and activist Martin Luther King, Jr. rose to prominence as the movement's most prominent voice and leader. He worked for the rights of Black Americans as well as other minority groups in the United States via the use of peaceful resistance and civil disobedience to fight racial discrimination and segregation laws.

The "I Have a Dream" speech, which King gave in 1963 on the steps of the Lincoln Memorial in Washington, D.C., became a renowned turning point in the Civil Rights Movement and a potent representation of the fight for equality and justice. In his address, Martin Luther King Jr. demanded an end to racism and discrimination, as well as a society in which individuals are assessed not by the color of their skin but by the quality of their character.

King's advocacy and visionary leadership sparked a flurry of peaceful protests and civil liberties marches throughout the nation, notably the Selma to Montgomery and Montgomery Bus Boycott marches. The 1964 Civil Rights Act and the 1965 Voting Rights Act, which helped end legal discrimination and segregation and guaranteed that all Americans, irrespective of race, had the right to vote, were both passed with his support.

Martin Luther King Jr. was a man of profound faith, unflinching bravery, and limitless compassion. He devoted his life to the pursuit of equality and justice, and his vision continues to motivate people worldwide to strive for a more fair and equitable society. He is widely considered one of the most influential personalities in the global fight for human rights and one of the finest leaders in American history.

Question 84: Which movement sought to eliminate racial discrimination?

Explanation: The Movement for Civil Rights was the movement that sought to eradicate racial discrimination. In the United States, the Movement for Civil Rights was a political and social movement that aimed to remove discrimination and segregation against African Americans as well as other minority groups. During the mid-1950s through the late-1960s, the movement was marked by civil disobedience, peaceful resistance, and other types of direct action.

Rosa Parks, Martin Luther King, Jr. and others led the Civil Rights Movement, which aimed to challenge the present framework of discrimination and segregation by a variety of measures, including marches, demonstrations, and legal challenges. The movement's efforts resulted in a number of significant legal and political developments, notably the enactment of the 1964 Civil Rights act and the 1965 Voting Rights, which helped to end legal segregation and guarantee the ability to vote for all Americans, regardless of ethnicity.

In addition to having a tremendous effect on American culture and society, the Civil Rights Movement inspired individuals all over the world to struggle for a more just and equal society. Today, the movement is considered one of the most significant political and social movements in American history, and it continues to serve as a source of inspiration and a call to action for people attempting to address current concerns of inequality, discrimination, and social justice.

Question 85: What was the United States' principal preoccupation throughout the Cold War?

Explanation: The United States' primary worry throughout the Cold War was the rise of communism. From the end of The Second World war in 1945 until the early nineties, the Cold War was an era of economic, political, and military friction between the US and its allies and the Soviet Union and its allies. A fundamental dispute on the nature of economic systems, government, and global power was at the heart of the struggle.

The United States viewed communism, as practiced by the Soviet Union and other nations, as a danger to its democratic and capitalist ideals and feared the expansion of communism to other nations. The United States viewed the Soviet Union's attempts to spread communism by supporting communist organizations and governments in many nations as a direct threat to American power and influence.

As a result, the US implemented a containment policy intended to prevent communism from spreading to other nations. This policy featured a blend of economic, diplomatic, and military actions, including the formation of military alliances, the employment of economic aid, and the placement of US military personnel in various regions of the globe.

Fear of communism's growth contributed to a number of key events during the Cold War, including the Vietnam War, the Korean War, and the Cuban Missile Crisis, as well as considerable military and political friction between the US and the Soviet Union. Despite these obstacles, the United States remained dedicated to preventing the expansion of communism throughout the Cold War, and the Soviet Union's fall in 1991 marked the end of this period in American history.

Question 86: Prior to becoming president, Eisenhower served as a general. Which war did he participate in?

Explanation: Before becoming president, Dwight D. Eisenhower served in World War II as a general. During World War II, Eisenhower was the Supreme Allied Commander in Europe and received several decorations for his service. In this capacity, he was responsible for directing the victorious Allied campaign in Europe, which eventually led to the defeat of Nazi Germany and the conclusion of the war in Europe.

Eisenhower's command and strategic abilities during World War II served to position him as one of the most influential military commanders of his age and made him a national hero. He maintained his military career after the war, rising to the rank of Supreme Commander of NATO before leaving the military to enter politics.

Eisenhower campaigned for president as the Republican nominee in 1952 and was elected, serving two terms as the 34th President of the USA from 1953 to 1961. Throughout his presidency, he continued to exhibit his leadership abilities and his dedication to the defense of the US and its alliances, and he was instrumental in the nation's reaction to the Cold War's difficulties.

Question 87: Who did the U.S. battle during World War II?

Explanation: During World War Two, the United States battled the Axis forces, which consisted of Italy, Germany, and Japan.

In Europe, the war began in 1939, when Germany, led by its ruler Adolf Hitler, attacked Poland. In the subsequent years, Germany rapidly captured a large portion of Europe, notably France and the low nations, and constituted a substantial danger to the region's stability and security.

As a response to the aggressiveness of the Central powers, the US joined arms with the Alliance, which included the United Kingdom, the Soviet Union, and several other nations. These nations collaborated to overthrow the Axis forces and establish security and peace throughout Europe and around the globe.

With the Japanese attack on the US naval station at Hawaii's Pearl Harbor on December 7, 1941, the US entered the war. This strike drew the US into the conflict on the allied side, and American soldiers fought alongside their partners in both the European and Pacific theatres.

The war was defined by some of the greatest and bloodiest engagements in human history, including, among others, the D-Day assault of Normandy, the Battle of Stalingrad, and the War of Midway. The United States and its allies finally prevailed over the Axis powers, ending World War II and clearing the way for a new age of global cooperation and peace.

3.3 Integrated Civics

A: Geography

Question 88: What body of water is located on the US East coast States?

Explanation: The Atlantic Ocean is the ocean on the US East coast States. The Atlantic Ocean is a large body of salt water that stretches from the Arctic Ocean to the Antarctic Ocean, dividing the Americas from Africa and Europe. The Atlantic Ocean is surrounded by several nations and is a vital maritime route for the world economy, linking major ports and cities.

The Atlantic Ocean is a significant source of entertainment and tourism in the United States, as well as an essential home for several marine animals. The ocean offers a number of ecological services, along with being a key source of food and income for many coastal areas, and it also regulates the temperature and weather patterns of the planet.

Question 89: What ocean is located on the United States West Coast?

Explanation: The Pacific Ocean is the ocean on the West Coast of the US. The Pacific Ocean is the world's biggest and deepest oceanic division, covering more than Sixty million square miles. The Pacific Ocean surrounds the West Coast of the United States and runs from (west) Asia and Australia to the (east) Americas, as well as from the Arctic Ocean to the Southern Ocean.

Question 90: Identify one of the United States two longest rivers.

Explanation: The Missouri River is one of the 2 longest rivers in the US. From its source in Montana's Rocky Mountains to its ending point at the Mississippi River in St. Louis, Missouri, the Missouri River is an impressive 2,341 miles in length. It is one of the largest rivers in the US and a vital supplier of water for several states, including North Dakota, Iowa, Montana, South Dakota, Kansas, Nebraska, Missouri, and Illinois.

The Mississippi River is the United States' other longest river. From Lake Itasca in Minnesota to the Gulf of Mexico, the Mississippi River stretches for roughly 2,320 miles. It is the 4th longest river in the world and one of the most significant waterways in the United States, offering transportation, water supplies, and recreational possibilities to the people who live along its banks.

Question 91: Identify one of the states bordering Mexico.

Explanation: California is one of the states that border Mexico. California is situated on the west coast of the USA and shares a border with Sonora and Baja California, both of which are located in Mexico. The international border between Mexico and California stretches around 140 miles from the Pacific Ocean to the Colorado River Delta in the east. The most populous state in the USA is California, and it is noted for its diversified topography, which includes the Sierra Nevada mountain range, the agricultural region of the Central Valley, and the Pacific coastline.

Question 92: State that shares a border with Canada.

Explanation: Alaska is one of the states that border Canada. Alaska is the biggest state in the USA in terms of land area, and it shares an eastern border with British Columbia. Pacific Ocean to the Arctic Ocean, the international border between Canada and Alaska spans roughly 1,538 miles. Alaska is renowned for its rough, wild beauty and enormous natural resources, such as natural gas, oil, and minerals. Alaska is also home to some of the state's most stunning national parks, including Denali National Park and Preserve, as well as its distinctive species, including caribou, moose, and grizzly bears.

Question 93: Name an American territory.

Explanation: Puerto Rico is a territory of the United States. Puerto Rico is a United States unincorporated territory situated in the Caribbean Sea. Located west of the Virgin Islands, and east of the Dominican Republic, it is an archipelago consisting of one main island and numerous smaller islands. Puerto Rico is a self-governing territory that has its own constitution, and its population is American citizens, yet they have no voting representation in the United States Congress. El Yunque National Forest is the only tropical rainforest in the United States National Forest System, and the island as a whole is famous for its rich cultural legacy, vibrant dance and music traditions, and gorgeous beaches and natural features.

Question 94: What is the location of the Statue of Liberty?

Explanation: On Liberty Island in the New York Harbor in New York City, stands the Statue of Liberty. On October 28, 1886, the French people gave the monument to the United States as a gift. Because of its importance as a representation of democracy and liberty, the Statue of Liberty has grown to become one of the most recognisable symbols in the United States. Along with its pedestal, the statue stands 305 feet tall and depicts a robed woman who represents Libertas, the Roman goddess of liberty, while holding a torch and a tablet aloft in her left hand. The National Park Service is in charge of overseeing the Statue of Liberty's management as a National Monument as part of the Liberty Statue Ellis Island and National Monument.

Question 95: What is the name of the United States' capital?

Explanation: The capital city of the United States is Washington, D.C. The capital and administrative hub of the country is Washington, DC, which is a part of the District of Columbia. Washington, DC is a federal district that is surrounded by the states of Virginia and Maryland and is situated in the northeastern region of the country along the Potomac River. Washington, D.C., which bears the name of the country's first president, George Washington, is the location of several of the most recognizable buildings and monuments in the country, including the Washington Monument, the Lincoln Memorial, the White House, and the U.S. Capitol. Washington, D.C., is home to several prominent universities and research institutions in addition to a number of galleries, museums, and cultural organizations.

B: Symbols

Question 96: What is the national anthem called?

Explanation: The US's national anthem is titled "The Star-Spangled Banner" written by Francis Scott Key. A congressional act formally recognized it as the national anthem in 1931. The War of 1812 is reflected in the lyrics, particularly the successful defense of Fort McHenry against a British attack. The hymn's four verses and chorus are frequently performed by Americans on patriotic events, and its music is adapted from the English classic "To Anacreon in Heaven." The opening stanza is the one that is most frequently recited.

Question 97: Why are there 13 stripes on the flag?

Explanation: The thirteen stripes on the American flag commemorate the thirteen original colonies that claimed independence from Britain and founded the United States of America. Every stripe symbolizes one of the original 13 colonies and reflects the unification of the original 13 states. The flag was designed in 1777 by the Continental Congress, and it has seen various modifications as new states entered the union through the years. The current layout of the flag, consisting of thirteen white and red stripes and a blue background with fifty white stars signifying the fifty states, was approved on July 4, 1960, after Hawaii became the 50th state. The stars and stripes on the flag are intended to symbolize the strength and solidarity of the

American people, and it is widely known as a representation of the United States and its principles of freedom, liberty, and justice.

Question 98: Why are there fifty stars on the flag?

Explanation: The 50 stars on the flag of the USA reflect the fifty states that make up the nation. As more states have been admitted to the union, the amount of stars on the flag has altered over time. In 1777, when the flag was initially created, it included 13 stars to signify the 13 founding colonies that claimed autonomy from Britain and subsequently established the USA. As the nation grew and additional states were added, the number of stars on the flag rose to symbolize the nation's rising size. The present design of the flag, which consists of 50 stars organized in a design of 9 lines of stars scattered horizontally and 11 lines of stars staggered vertically, was chosen on July 4, 1960, when Hawaii became the 50th state. The fifty stars on the American flag represent the unity and variety of the American people and are widely recognized as a symbol of the United States and its ideals of freedom, liberty, and justice.

C: Holidays

Question 99: Name two U.S. national holidays.

Explanation: There are numerous national holidays celebrated in the US, but the two most prominent are:

Independence Day entails. This holiday commemorates the signing of the Independence Declaration on July 4, 1776, which proclaimed the freedom of the thirteen colonies from British authority. Americans commemorate this day with parades, picnics, and fireworks.

Thanksgiving Day is observed annually on the fourth Thursday of November to commemorate the first bountiful harvest and meal shared by the Wampanoag Native Americans and

Pilgrims in 1621. On this day, Americans offer gratitude for their blessings and share a celebratory lunch with family and friends.

These two holidays, along with others such as Labor Day, Memorial Day, and Presidents' Day, are recognized by the federal government as official holidays, and many Americans observe them.

Question 100: When is Independence Day celebrated?

Explanation: Independence Day, often known as the 4th of July, is annually observed on July 4 in the United States. The Declaration of Independence, which declared the 13 colonies' independence from British sovereignty, was signed on July 4, 1776, and is commemorated by this holiday. On this day, Americans celebrate with picnics, parades, and fireworks; it is regarded as one of the most significant public holidays in the United States. Independence Day is a moment for Americans to focus on their nation's history, legacy, and principles, as well as to celebrate the liberties and possibilities that make the US a great nation.

CHAPTER 4: CIVICS PRACTICE TEST Q&A

This test consists of ten random questions from the official USCIS Naturalization exam. You must properly answer at least six questions to pass. Cover the green section and take the exam!

Test Questions	Correct Answers
Our Constitution grants the federal government certain authorities. What is one of the federal government's powers?	✓ to declare war ✓ to make treaties ✓ to print money ✓ to create an army ✓
The Federalist Papers advocated for the adoption of the United States Constitution. Mention one of the authors.	✓ Publius ✓ Alexander Hamilton ✓ James Madison ✓ John Jay
What does "the rule of law" mean?	✓ Leaders must obey the law ✓ No one is above the law ✓ Everyone must follow the law ✓ Government must obey the law
Name one war waged by the United States in the nineteenth century.	✓ Mexican-American War ✓ War of 1812 ✓ Spanish-American War ✓ Civil War
Our Constitution grants the federal government certain authorities. What is one of the federal government's powers?	✓ to declare war ✓ to make treaties

	✓ to print money ✓ to create an army
What ocean is located on the United States West Coast?	✓ Pacific Ocean
How many United States Senators exist?	✓ One Hundred (100)
What is the location of the Statue of Liberty?	✓ Liberty Island ✓ New York (Harbor)
When was the United States Constitution written?	✓ 1787
State that shares a border with Mexico.	✓ Texas ✓ Arizona ✓ California ✓ New Mexico

CHAPTER 5: EXCEPTIONS

A candidate may be eligible for an exemption from the civics or English requirement or both. The chart below provides a fast reference for the exceptions to the naturalization requirements for English and civics.

Exceptions	Civics: Familiarity with the U.S. government and history	English: Read, speak, write, and understand
At the time of filing, be at least 50 years old and have been a legal permanent resident (LPR) for more than 20 years.	Still necessary. Candidates may take the civics exam in their native language with the assistance of an interpreter.	Exempt
At the time of filing, be at least 55 years old and have lived in the US as an LPR for at least fifteen years.	Still necessary. Candidates may take the civics exam in their native language with the assistance of an interpreter.	Exempt
At the time of filing, be at least 65 years old and have lived in the US as an LPR for at minimum 20 years.	Officers continue to administer specifically marked exam forms. Candidates may take the civics exam in their preferred language with the assistance of an interpreter.	Exempt
Medical Condition Exemption	It may be excused from civics, English, or both.	It may be excused from civics, English, or both.

5.1 Civics Exam Special Considerations

An applicant receives particular attention on the civics exam if, at the time the application is filed, the applicant is at least 65 years old and has resided in the United States for at least 20 years following legal admission as a permanent resident. Applicants who qualify for special consideration are given specialized examination forms.

5.2 Residence And Age Exemption To English

A candidate is excluded from the English language test but must still encounter the civics requirement if:

- The applicant is over 50 years old at the time of applying for naturalization and has been an LPR for at least 20 years; or

- The candidate is age 55 or over at the time of applying for naturalization and has been an LPR for at least 15 years.

The candidate may take the civics exam in the language of his or her choosing with the assistance of an interpreter.

5.3 English And Civics Exemption For Medical Disabilities

A candidate with a medical impairment who cannot fulfill the English and civics requirements may be excluded from the English and civics requirement or both.

5.4 Compliance With IRCA 1986 Requirements

In order to be eligible for adjustment to LPR status, the Immigration Reform and Control Act of 1986 (IRCA) stipulated that individuals authorized under INA 245A must fulfill a threshold for basic citizenship skills.

- Passing standardised civics and English tests provided by organisations that were once recognised by the INS;

- Passing tests in English and civics administered by the previous Naturalization and Immigration Service (INS).

At the time of the re-examination for naturalization, the officer solely re-examines the applicant on any component of the exam that the candidate did not pass in accordance with IRCA. At the time of the naturalization examination, all applicants must demonstrate their ability to speak English unless they fulfill one of the time and age as resident exemptions for English or qualify for a medical waiver.

CHAPTER 6: TEST MATERIAL

Here is some important test material to help you study for the US citizenship test.

6.1 History Of USA

The United States is a federal republic comprised of 50 states in North America. In addition to the 48 contiguous states that occupy the main latitudes of the continent, the US consists of Alaska, located in the far northwest of North America, and Hawaii, an island state in the center of the Pacific Ocean. The contiguous states are bordered by Canada to the north, the Atlantic Ocean to the east, the Gulf of Mexico and Mexico to the south, and the Pacific Ocean to the west. The United States ranks fourth in the world in terms of land area (after China, Canada, and Russia). Washington is the nation's capital, and the whole District of Columbia (which was established in 1791) is considered to be part of the city.

United States of America

Maybe the most notable attribute of the United States is its vast diversity. Its physical environment spans from arctic to subtropical, from lush rain forest to dry desert, and from rocky mountain top to flat plain. Although the United States has a huge population by international standards, its population density is comparatively low. The country encompasses some of the world's greatest urban densities as well as some of the largest expanses that are nearly empty of human inhabitants.

The United States has a population that is quite diversified. In contrast to China, which primarily assimilated indigenous individuals, the United States' diversity is mostly the result of massive and continuous worldwide immigration. The United States likely possesses a greater diversity of ethnic, racial, and cultural groups than any other nation. In addition to the descendants of Africans brought as slaves to the New World and the remaining Native Americans (including Aleuts, American Indians, and Eskimos), the hundreds of millions of immigrants who have migrated to America in search of better political, social, and economic possibilities than they had in the areas they left have enriched, challenged, and continuously redefined the country's character. (It must be emphasized that although the phrases "America" and "Americans" are frequently used as synonyms for the U. S. and its residents, they are also used in a wider scope to refer to South, North, and Central America and its citizens.)

In terms of total domestic output, the United States has the biggest economic influence in the world (GDP). The nation's prosperity is somewhat attributable to its abundant natural resources and massive agricultural production, but it is primarily due to its highly developed industry. Due to the sheer scale of its economy, the United States is the most influential single force in international commerce, despite its relative economic independence in many sectors. Its imports and exports contribute significantly to the global total. The United States influences the world economy as both a provider and a recipient of investment money. The nation continues to maintain a more diverse economy than any other on Globe, giving the majority of its citizens one of the greatest standards of living in the world.

6.2 American Government

The United States is a federal constitutional republic, which implies that power is shared between a centralized power (the federal government) and component political subdivisions (the states). The United States Constitution, which was ratified in 1787 and is the supreme law of the land, describes the organization and powers of the federal government and explains the fundamental ideas and liberties upon which the nation was created.

Legislative, judicial and executive branches comprise the 3 branches of the government.

The legislative branch is accountable for lawmaking. Each state is given two senators in the Senate, while the population determines representation in the House of Representatives. The legislative body has the authority to enact legislation, ratify nominees and agreements, and approve the government budget.

The executive branch is accountable for law enforcement. The American president is elected for a 4-year term and is the potential for reelection for a second term. The President is aided by the Vice President and a Cabinet of advisors who are in charge of the executive departments. In addition to the military and several autonomous organizations, such as the Federal Bureau of Investigation and the Central Intelligence Agency (CIA), the executive branch also comprises the military (FBI).

The judiciary is responsible for the interpretation of legislation. It consists of a network of federal judges, with the Supreme Court of the US serving as the nation's highest court. The Supreme Court has the authority of judicial review, which allows it to declare unlawful legislation that violates the Constitution.

Federalism, checks and balances and separation of powers are the guiding concepts of the American political system. Federalism guarantees that every government level has a responsibility in running the country by dividing authority between the federal and state governments. Separation of powers separates the government's powers across the three parts, while checks and balances prevent any one branch from becoming too dominant by permitting each department to limit the other branches' powers.

The U.S. has a system of state and municipal governments, each with its own responsibilities and authorities, in addition to the federal government. Local governments are responsible for problems such as land use, zoning, and local taxation, whereas state governments are responsible for topics such as public safety, education, and transportation.

Citizens are able to engage in the political system by voting and holding elected officials responsible for their actions. In addition to being founded on the rule of law, the government is a constitutional republic, which implies that the laws and the Constitution of the nation limit the government's powers and safeguard the rights and freedoms of individuals.

6.3 Principles Of American Democracy

The fundamentals of American democracy are the fundamental concepts and ideals upon which the American political system is founded. These principles contribute to defining the nation's character and guiding the conduct of its inhabitants and elected authorities. Some of the most significant concepts of American democracy are as follows:

- **Popular sovereignty**: The individuals are the primary part of the political power in the US, according to the idea of popular sovereignty. The government is founded by and responsible to the people. This value is mirrored in the democratic system, which grants citizens the ability to cast ballots and engage in politics.

- **Limited government**: This theory asserts that the Constitution and the laws of the country restrict the authority of the government. The government is not omnipotent; rather, it is subject to limits established to preserve the rights and liberties of individuals.

- **Separation of powers**: This concept stipulates that the government's powers are split between the executive, legislative, and judicial departments. This separation of powers prevents any one arm of government from being too dominant and guarantees that the multiple branches of government may serve as checks and balances for one another.

- **Federalism**: This idea stipulates that the states and federal government share authority. The federal government has some authority, like the ability to regulate trade and support national defense, while the states have many other powers, including the ability to control education and manage local taxation.

- **Individual rights and freedoms**: According to this idea, the government must defend the fundamental rights and liberties of its citizens, such as freedom of religion, speech, and the press. The Bill of Rights, which consists of the first 10 modifications to the Constitution, elaborates on fundamental rights and liberties.

- **Majority rule and minority rights:** This idea emphasizes that the government is built on the principle of the rule of the majority while protecting the rights of minorities. The government must protect the rights of all people, regardless of their minority status, and guarantee that the majority does not violate the rights of minorities.

- **The rule of law**: The rule of law states that the law serves equally to all individuals and that the government must operate within the bounds of the law.

The rule of law facilitates government accountability and civilian access to justice.

- **Political equality**: This concept argues that all residents have an equal opportunity to engage in the democratic process and have their opinions heard. The freedom to vote, which is a basic right in American democracy, reflects political equality.

Fundamental tenets of American democracy are enshrined in the Constitution, which outlines the fundamental framework of the government and the rights and liberties of individuals. The democratic system, through which voters may engage in the political system and hold elected officials responsible for their acts, also reflects the values. The fundamentals of American democracy guarantee that the US continues to be a representative, rule-of-law-based democracy that safeguards the rights and liberties of all citizens.

6.4 System Of Government

As the United States operates under a federal system, authority is shared between the federal and state levels. Because of this separation of powers, citizens are held responsible by the government and have a voice in policymaking.

There are three distinct parts to the national government: the legislature, the executive, and the judiciary.

Laws are created by the House of Representatives and the Senate, which make up the legislative branch. Each state has two senators, whereas the number of representatives is proportional to its population in the House of Representatives. The legislative arm of government is in charge of making the rules and regulations for the country and monitoring the actions of the executive and judicial branches.

The President serves as both the nation's chief executive and its chief law enforcement officer, making him the undisputed leader of the executive branch. The President can veto legislation that Congress has enacted and appoints judges and other government employees. It is the President's responsibility to lead the country's armed forces.

The judicial branch includes both the federal Supreme Court and the federal district courts. The nine judges of the Supreme Court are selected by the President and ratified by the Senate, making it the highest court in the nation. The judicial system is in charge of applying legal precedent and checking on government and citizen compliance with the Constitution.

Moreover, each state is governed by its own government with authority to legislate and execute laws inside its borders. The Constitution, however, grants the federal government the authority to supersede state laws under certain conditions.

Because of this structure of checks and balances, any part of the government in the United States can constrain the authority of any other branch. To provide just two examples, the legislature may overturn a veto by the president with a two-thirds vote, whereas the judiciary can rule that legislation approved by Congress is unconstitutional.

Having a government that answers to its citizens, respects their rights and liberties, and acts in their best interests is a key feature of this form of government. Citizens of the United States, like in any other democratic nation, have the responsibility to hold their representatives to account for the decisions they make after they are in office.

6.5 Rights And Responsibilities

There are privileges and duties that come with becoming a U.S. citizen.

Freedom of expression, religion, assembly, press, and petition are all guaranteed to you.

The right to keep and bear arms; the right to privacy; the right to vote; the right to equal treatment under the law; the right to a fair trial;

These guarantees may be found in the first 10 amendments to the United States Constitution, known as the Bill of Rights. They protect individuals' fundamental liberties and rights and restrict the government's ability to infringe on such protections.

As a citizen, you have not only rights but also obligations. Some examples of these duties are:

- Honoring the freedoms and rights of others; paying taxes; obeying the law; serving in the military if called upon; participating in the political process by voting and remaining informed about public issues; and serving on a jury if summoned all fall under the umbrella of citizenship.

- You can assist in keeping our democracy and civil order robust by carrying out these duties. And by becoming involved in politics and holding your representatives to account, you can help guarantee that your liberties will continue to be safeguarded.

- The Constitution safeguards your rights, but it also places some restrictions on those rights. Even if you have freedom of speech, you cannot use it to advocate violence or spread false information with the intent to hurt others. In the same way, the right to carry arms does not preclude the government from imposing reasonable restrictions on the ownership and use of weapons for the sake of public security.

- As a citizen, you have certain rights and obligations that are fundamental to the functioning of the United States' democratic government. Maintaining a robust and democratic society for yourself and future generations depends on upholding and defending these rights and obligations.

6.6 Colonial Period And Independence

Colonization in the United States occurred from the late sixteenth century until the mid-18th century, during which time European settlers built colonies in North America. In 1607, the first prosperous British colony was founded in the present-day state of Virginia at Jamestown. For the following 150 years, the British settled what would become 13 colonies along the East

Coast of North America, the Spanish built colonies in the Southwest and South, and the French settled the Great Lakes and the area around the Mississippi River.

At this time, the colonies were under the direct control of the British government and their economy was based mostly on trade and agriculture. Even while the colonists established their own ways of life and economies, they were nonetheless bound by the rules and regulations of a British government that was distant and unfamiliar with their situation.

During the middle of the 18th century, taxation, trade limitations, and limits on colonial autonomy were all contributing factors to growing tensions between the British government and colonists. Stamp Act, passed by the British Parliament in 1765, levied a tax on any printed matter, including newspapers and legal documents, produced in the American colonies. The colonists protested and resisted because they saw this as an unfair attack on their liberties.

The American Revolutionary War broke out in 1775 when tensions between the colonists and the British finally reached a breaking point. In 1776, the colonies signed the Declaration of Independence, officially declaring their independence from Britain. The colonists, backed by France and other allies, struggled for independence for several years and eventually triumphed.

By signing the Treaty of Paris in 1783, the British and French formally acknowledged American independence and declared the War of Independence over. After establishing a new federal form of government and guaranteeing fundamental rights and freedoms to its inhabitants, the new nation went on to design and adopt the Constitution.

The struggle for independence from Britain and the subsequent establishment of a new nation were watershed milestones in American history. The United States became a global leader after its successful fight for independence, and the installation of a democratic system inspired similar movements in other countries. Colonialism and the subsequent American Revolution left an indelible mark on American culture and politics that has yet to fade fully.

6.7 1800s

The 19th century, or the 1800s, was a time of tremendous development and expansion for the United States. The country grew in territory and population and experienced profound shifts in its economic, social, and political landscape throughout this time.

In 1803, the United States acquired a considerable chunk of the land that is now the American Midwest from France. This acquisition, known as the Louisiana Purchase, is widely regarded as one of the most important events of the 1800s. The

land mass that may now be developed or settled was effectively doubled as a result of this purchase.

The United States likewise had a time of rapid industrialization in the late 1800s, when new technologies and inventions radically altered the country's economic landscape. There were several contributors to this expansion, including an increase in the available labor and in the amount of money available for investments and the exploitation of natural resources.

The lengthy and bitter fight over slavery in America was finally resolved in 1865 with the end of the Civil War, which occurred in the 1800s. The end of slavery was a watershed moment in American history, one that prepared the way for the ultimate extension of civil liberties and legal protections to all residents regardless of their color.

In addition to these milestones, the 1800s also witnessed the westward push of American settlers as they colonized uncharted territory. Its growth was prompted by people's pursuit of wealth, power, and adventure.

To sum up, the 1800s were a time of tremendous development and expansion for the United States, and they set the stage for the country's subsequent growth and success.

6.8 Facts About Current American History And Other Historical Events

The term "recent American history" is used to describe the period of time beginning in the early 20th century and ending in the present day. There have been many noteworthy developments and occurrences during this time in American history.

First and foremost, the United States' participation in both World Wars I and II had far-reaching consequences for both the world and the country.

The Great Depression was an economic crisis that hit the United States hard in the late 1920s and early 1930s. During a time of economic difficulty, the government implemented a number of initiatives and reforms aimed at reviving the country's economy.

In the middle of the 20th century, American minorities, including African Americans, started to call for equal legal protections and rights. Nonviolent demonstrations, civil disobedience, and other types of activity defined this movement, which was pivotal in bringing about the Civil Rights Act of 1964.

In the years after World War II, the US and the Soviet Union fought a global conflict for military and political supremacy known as the Cold War. Several facets of American society and

international policy were impacted by the period of heightened tension and war.

The United States has undergone a technical revolution in recent decades that has altered the ways in which people there interact with one another, perform their jobs, and get access to information. As the Web and other forms of technology have advanced, they have had far-reaching effects on American culture and the worldwide economy.

The evolution of the American judicial and political systems, as well as the founding and early history of the United States, the American Revolution, and the construction of the Constitution, may also be covered on a citizenship exam. Applicants for citizenship may also be expected to demonstrate familiarity with fundamentals such as American history and government.

Democracy and the supremacy of law are the bedrock of the American government. Power is shared between the federal govt and the various states under this arrangement, known as a "federal system of government."

In the American political system, executive, legislative, and judicial authorities are well delineated from one another. Each department of government has a specific function: the legislature makes laws, the administration enforces them, and the courts interpret them.

To comprehend the powers and structure of the state, as well as the protections and rights granted to the American people, one must go no further than The Constitution of the US, the supreme law of the nation. Freedom of religion, speech, and the press are only a few of the individual liberties guaranteed by the first 10 amendments to the United States Constitution, known as the Bill of Rights.

The ability to vote and take part in government is fundamental to American democracy. Each American citizen over the age of eighteen is eligible to vote and run for public office, as well as take part in the electoral process, town hall meetings, and other political activities.

All citizens of the United States have the right to vote and participate in government, but they also have the duty to pay taxes, serve on juries, and uphold the law. Also, they should be active members of their communities and sensitive to the rights and liberties of others around them.

Colonial America is the historical era during which the original British colonies in North America were founded and expanded. During the course of many centuries, the colonies flourished, but by the late 1700s, many colonists felt oppressed by British authority.

In the late 1700s and early 1800s, a chain of events known as the American Revolution resulted in the Thirteen British colonies in North America declaring their independence from

Britain and uniting to establish the United States of America. The American colonists battled against the British army in the Revolutionary War, and the Americans finally prevailed and created the nation of the U.S. as a result.

A lot happened in the United States in the 1800s. When pioneers and settlers headed west, the United States grew. Manufacturing and trade expanded during the 1800s, and new transportation and technology networks were established during this time. In addition, the 1800s were a tense decade as the country fought to find solutions to divisive topics like slavery and state sovereignty.

6.9 Integrated Civics

Applicants seeking U.S. citizenship take an all-encompassing course called "Integrated Civics," which is designed to teach them about the American government, history, and culture. Integrated Civics is required for anyone seeking citizenship in the United States so that they may learn the ins and outs of American culture and society and be better prepared to participate in civic life once they become citizens.

The following are some of the most important parts of Integrated Civics that are examined in depth:

American democratic principles number one: This necessitates familiarity with concepts like equality, justice, liberty, and representative democracy, which are the bedrock of the American political system.

The second topic is "System of Government," and it entails learning about the workings of the federal government and its three branches (the Executive, the Congress, and the Courts).

The third pillar is titled "Rights and Duties of Citizenship," and it details the privileges and obligations of being a U.S. citizen, including the right to vote, freedom of speech and religion, due process, and jury duty. Citizen duties such as compliance with the law, financial support from the government, and active participation in elections are also addressed.

Topics covered in this branch of history include the Civil War, the American Revolution, and the Civil Rights Movement, to name a few.

Five, an appreciation for American norms, traditions, and cultural ideals such as equality, liberty, and the pursuit of joy.

Integrated Civics also includes lessons on the history of the English language, the process of citizenship, and the history and significance of major U.S. festivals and symbols. The curriculum places emphasis on teaching students vital skills, such as the English language, interpreting official documents, and political engagement.

One's grasp of the foundational ideals and concepts of American society can be enhanced via the study of Integrated Civics. Students learn what it takes to become contributing members of society and integral figures in American culture. Successful completion of Integrated Civics is a prerequisite for becoming a naturalized citizen of the United States.

6.10 Geography

The territories, states, and major cities of the United States, as well as their physical and political characteristics, are the primary subject of the citizenship test's geography section. Geography courses are designed to familiarise students with the layout of the United States and its political subdivisions.

Some of the most important questions in the U.S. citizenship test's geography section are as follows:

States and Capitals: This covers a study of the 50 states and capital cities of the United States. On a map, candidates are expected to recognize the states and their capitals.

Each of the fifty states in the United States has its own capital city. On the U.S. Citizenship Test, you may be asked to identify a state and its capital or to match a state with its capital. Following is a list of the 50 states and their capital cities in the United States of America.

1. Alaska – Juneau
2. Alabama - Montgomery
3. Arizona - Phoenix
4. California – Sacramento
5. Arkansas - Little Rock
6. Colorado - Denver
7. Delaware – Dover
8. Connecticut - Hartford
9. Florida - Tallahassee
10. Hawaii – Honolulu
11. Georgia - Atlanta
12. Idaho - Boise
13. Indiana – Indianapolis

14. Illinois - Springfield

15. Iowa - Des Moines

16. Kentucky – Frankfort

17. Kansas - Topeka

18. Louisiana - Baton Rouge

19. Maryland – Annapolis

20. Maine - Augusta

21. Massachusetts - Boston

22. Minnesota - Saint Paul

23. Michigan - Lansing

24. Mississippi - Jackson

25. Montana – Helena

26. Missouri - Jefferson City

27. Nebraska - Lincoln

28. New Hampshire – Concord

29. Nevada - Carson City

30. New Jersey - Trenton

31. New York – Albany

32. New Mexico - Santa Fe

33. North Carolina - Raleigh

34. Ohio – Columbus

35. North Dakota - Bismarck

36. Oklahoma - Oklahoma City

37. Pennsylvania – Harrisburg

38. Oregon - Salem

39. Rhode Island - Providence

40. South Dakota – Pierre

41. South Carolina - Columbia

42. Tennessee - Nashville

43. Utah - Salt Lake City

44. Texas - Austin

45. Wisconsin - Madison

46. Wyoming - Cheyenne

47. Vermont - Montpelier

48. Washington – Olympia

49. Virginia - Richmond

50. West Virginia - Charleston

Major Cities: This includes some of the most populous and significant cities in the United States, including Los Angeles, New York, and Chicago. Applicants must be capable of locating these cities on a map. Typically, "major cities" refers to cities that are notable in terms of population, cultural significance, economic activity, or political influence. Examples of important cities about which you may be questioned on the exam include:

- Los Angeles

- New York City

- San Jose

- Chicago

- Philadelphia

- Houston

- Phoenix

- San Diego

- San Antonio

- Dallas

It is a good idea to acquaint yourself with the locations and names of as many cities as possible, as the U.S. Citizenship Test may also inquire about additional cities that are deemed to be large. Moreover, you may be required to identify the state in which a big city is located; therefore, it is beneficial to have a thorough awareness of the United States geography.

Physical Features: This requires examining the United States' primary physical characteristics, such as its mountains, rivers, and deserts. On a map, candidates are required to recognize these features. Knowing the significance and location of these physical features is essential to comprehend the United States geography. Among the physical characteristics that you could be questioned about in the exam are the following:

- The Rocky Mountains

- The Mississippi River

- The Colorado River

- The Grand Canyon

- The Great Lakes (Huron, Erie, Superior, Michigan, and Ontario)

- The Mojave Desert

- The Appalachian Mountains

- The Hudson River

It is a good idea to acquaint yourself with as many of these qualities as possible, as the U.S. Citizenship Exam may also inquire about other physical characteristics that are relevant in the United States. Moreover, you may be asked to name the states in which various physical features are situated, so a broad awareness of the United States geography is also advantageous.

Political Divisions: This section describes the political divisions of the United States, including its states, territories, and capital city. On a map, candidates must be able to find these divisions. Each of the fifty states in the United States has its own constitution and set of laws. In addition, many territories, such as the U.S. Virgin Islands and Puerto Rico, are regarded to be a part of the United States but lack the same degree of political sovereignty as the states.

The United States federal government is divided into 3 branches: the executive branch (which executes the laws), the legislative branch (which makes the laws), and the judiciary branch (which interprets the laws) (which interprets the laws).

In the US Citizenship Exam, you might be given questions such as:

- What is the number of states in the United States?

- What is a certain state's capital?

- What is the function of the federal government's legislative branch?

- What is the president's position in the executive branch of the United States government?

To adequately prepare for the US Citizenship Test, it is essential to research and comprehends the United States' political differences.

Bodies of Water: This covers an examination of the major bodies of water around the United States, including the Pacific Ocean, the Atlantic Ocean, and the Gulf of Mexico. On a map, individuals are expected to recognize these bodies of water. The United States is bordered by several major bodies of water and has numerous notable rivers and lakes. The following bodies of water may be found in the United States:

Oceans:

- Gulf of Mexico

- Pacific Ocean

- Atlantic Ocean

Lakes:

- Huron

- Superior

- Michigan

- Lake of the Woods

- Ontario

- Erie

- Lake Champlain

- Lake Tahoe

- Lake Powell

- Crater Lake

- Lake Mead

Rivers:

- Colorado River

- Mississippi River

- Tennessee River

- Missouri River

- Snake River

- Ohio River

- Columbia River

- Arkansas River

- Rio Grande

- Hudson River

In addition to the topics listed above, the geography portion of the U.S. citizenship exam may contain questions concerning the location of other nations and their capitals in relation to the United States.

Individuals obtain a better grasp of the political and physical configuration of the United States and its position in the globe via the study of geography. This information is essential for those pursuing U.S. citizenship since it enables them to comprehend the country and its areas and become knowledgeable, engaged members of American society.

6.11 Symbols

From the perspective of the US Citizenship Test, it is essential to grasp the emblems of the United States, as these symbols embody the country's history, values, and culture. On the exam, you may be questioned about the following symbols:

The American flag

Patriotism and freedom, and independence are represented by the American flag.

The bald eagle

The bald eagle is the national emblem of the United States, representing power, independence, and national pride.

The Great Seal of the United States

The Great Seal of the United States appears on official papers such as passports and banknotes. It depicts an eagle with a shield and a flag in its beak.

The Statue of Liberty

The Statue of Liberty is a symbol of liberty, democracy, and optimism for people throughout the world.

The Pledge of Allegiance

The Pledge of Allegiance is repeated daily by millions of Americans as a symbol of commitment and patriotism.

The National Anthem

The National Anthem, "The Star-Spangled Banner," is performed at athletic events, national holidays, and other special occasions as a symbol of American patriotism.

On the US Citizenship Exam, you may be given questions on American symbols, such as:

- What does the American flag represent?

- What is the United States national bird?

- What is the United States Great Seal?

- What does the Liberty Statue represent?

To study for the US Citizenship Exam, it is essential to study and comprehend the national emblems of the United States.

6.12 Holidays

From the perspective of the US Citizenship Exam, it is essential to comprehend the holidays observed in the US. Holidays are significant because they represent the nation's history, beliefs, and culture and bring people together to celebrate and recognize significant events and individuals.

During the US Citizenship Exam, you may be asked about the following holidays:

Martin Luther King Jr. Day	January's 3rd Monday
Christmas Day	25th December
Memorial Day	May's last Monday
Labor Day	September's 1st Monday
Columbus Day	October's 2nd Monday
Thanksgiving Day	November's 4th Thursday
Independence Day	July 4th
Presidents' Day	February's 3rd Monday
New Year's Day	1st January
Veterans Day	November 11th

During the US Citizenship Test, you may be asked about holidays, such as:

- What is the importance of Martin Luther King Jr. Day?

- When is Veterans Day observed?

- What is Independence Day's significance?

- When is the Christmas holiday observed?

To adequately prepare for the US Citizenship Exam, it is essential to review and comprehend the holidays observed in the United States.

CONCLUSION

The US Citizenship Exam is an integral part of the naturalization procedure for becoming a United States citizen. The purpose of the examination is to evaluate the applicant's knowledge and comprehension of the US government, English language, culture and history.

To prepare for the exam, it is vital to study and comprehend important ideas and data, such as the three parts of government, the Constitution and the Bill of Rights, the political divisions of the US, significant cities, bodies of water, geographical characteristics, symbols, and festivals.

The US Citizenship Test includes ten questions drawn from a pool of 100, and in order to pass, candidates must answer at least six questions correctly. To qualify for citizenship, candidates must demonstrate a grasp of the English language, which is often assessed orally.

In addition to knowledge-based questions, the US Citizenship Test evaluates a candidate's capacity to assimilate into American culture. This involves a dedication to the Constitution's ideals, an awareness of American values, and a readiness to support and protect the nation.

Ultimately, the US Citizenship Test is a crucial component of the naturalization procedure, and it allows candidates to show their knowledge and awareness of the country they desire to call home. The exam is difficult, but anyone who prepares and works hard can pass and become a citizen of the United States.

To get access to you bonuses scan the secure QRcode below

Please note that the author of this book is not associated with any external links provided. Clicking on any links outside of this content may lead to websites or resources that are not controlled or endorsed by the author. Use caution when visiting external links and be sure to review their privacy policies and terms of use.

Made in the USA
Monee, IL
18 January 2024

52020299R00055